God So Close

EXPERIENCE
A LIFE AWAKENED
TO HIS SPIRIT

BECKY THOMPSON

W PUBLISHING GROUP

AN IMPRINT OF THOMAS NELSON

Published in Nashville, Tennessee, by W Publishing, an imprint of Thomas Nelson.

The author is represented by Alive Literary Agency, www.aliveliterary.com.

Thomas Nelson titles may be purchased in bulk for educational, business, fundraising, or sales promotional use. For information, please email SpecialMarkets@ThomasNelson.com.

Unless otherwise noted, Scripture quotations are taken from The Holy Bible, New International Version®, NIV®. Copyright © 1973, 1978, 1984, 2011 by Biblica, Inc.® Used by permission of Zondervan. All rights reserved worldwide. www.zondervan.com. The "NIV" and "New International Version" are trademarks registered in the United States Patent and Trademark Office by Biblica, Inc.®

Scripture quotations marked AMP are taken from the Amplified® Bible (AMP). Copyright © 2015 by The Lockman Foundation. Used by permission. www.lockman.org

Scripture quotations marked ESV are taken from the ESV® Bible (The Holy Bible, English Standard Version®). Copyright © 2001 by Crossway, a publishing ministry of Good News Publishers. Used by permission. All rights reserved.

Scripture quotations marked HCSB are taken from the Holman Christian Standard Bible®. Copyright © 1999, 2000, 2002, 2003, 2009 by Holman Bible Publishers. Used by permission. HCSB® is a federally registered trademark of Holman Bible Publishers.

Scripture quotations marked KJV are taken from the King James Version. Public domain.

Scripture quotations marked NKJV are taken from the New King James Version®. Copyright © 1982 by Thomas Nelson. Used by permission. All rights reserved.

Scripture quotations marked NLT are taken from the Holy Bible, New Living Translation. Copyright © 1996, 2004, 2015 by Tyndale House Foundation. Used by permission of Tyndale House Ministries, Carol Stream, Illinois 60188. All rights reserved.

All italics used in quoted Bible verses indicate emphasis added by the author.

Any internet addresses, phone numbers, or company or product information printed in this book are offered as a resource and are not intended in any way to be or to imply an endorsement by Thomas Nelson, nor does Thomas Nelson vouch for the existence, content, or services of these sites, phone numbers, companies, or products beyond the life of this book.

ISBN 97807852444318 (audiobook)
ISBN 9780785244417 (eBook)

Library of Congress Cataloging-in-Publication Data

ISBN 9780785244288

Printed in the United States of America
22 23 24 25 26   LSC   10 9 8 7 6 5 4 3 2 1

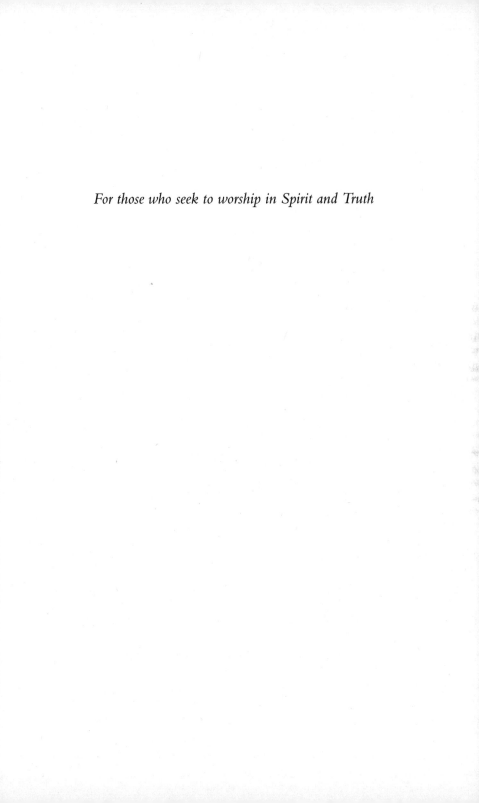

For those who seek to worship in Spirit and Truth

CONTENTS

CONTENTS

TO YOU, BEFORE WE BEGIN

I put my laptop on the kitchen table and opened a new document. As I sat facing the rolling green space behind my house in Tennessee, I thought about all I hoped this book would do once it reached you. So I pulled out two additional chairs at my table: one for you and the other for the Lord, because I wanted to remember that this is a conversation between friends. It looks like a book, but my prayer is that it reads like a transcript of a conversation over coffee.

Returning to my own chair, I took my seat behind my computer and prayed, *Lord, what do You want to say to her? What do You want to remind her of? What do You want to teach her? What do You want her to know about who You are?*

I waited, listening for His voice. *Becky, begin with love,* God answered. *Tell her it's because I love her that I made a way for us to be together. Tell her I sent My Son and My Spirit so I could be close to her just because I love her so much.*

I started to cry. It has always been love, hasn't it? We try to make our lives as followers of Jesus about so many things. But the foundation of all we believe is that the Father so loved us that He bought back our eternal relationship through the blood of Jesus. The Father so loved us that He wouldn't leave us orphans, and even after Jesus came and returned to heaven, He sent His Spirit so we could be together. *Love.*

So we'll start there, just as He prompted. My prayer for you is that before you read one more word, you will feel the presence of

God's love in the room with you. I don't know what your day has been like. I don't know what you've faced or even if it's morning, afternoon, or night as you read this. But I know this with full certainty: God is with you. Not in a cliché, *Yeah, Becky, of course God is with me; He's everywhere* kind of way. The Spirit of God is with you and wants to take all the cares you've been shouldering.

It's been a lot, hasn't it? Maybe everyone knows or maybe only God does, but what you've been walking through has been heavy. You need joy. You need peace. You need a good break and just not to be responsible for all the things anymore. My friend, what I can offer you is the reminder that the only one who can carry it all, take care of it all, and sort through all the details isn't distant or distracted. He's right here. Sometimes we forget that God has all the answers and He's right here with us.

Can we focus on His closeness for a second? Can we turn our hearts and attention on what it actually means that the same God who made all things is in the room with us right now? He's not a God who was only present and real during biblical times and has since set aside His power. He didn't form the earth and then step back, brushing the dust from creation off His hands, leaving us to figure out each day on our own. He's the God who sent His Son in the flesh and sent His Spirit into our hearts so He could walk each dusty day with us, washing off the worries of the world with the fresh, living water of His presence.

Do you sense Him reminding you of this truth? Take a deep breath, and let me pray for you.

Lord, melt away all the stress my friend has been carrying. Bring healing to any deep sadness in her heart. Help her sense Your love surrounding her now. In Jesus' name I pray. Amen.

You were made to be with Him. You weren't made to simply

know *about* God but to experience a relationship *with* Him—a relationship in which He is just as real to you now as He was in every story you've ever read about Him. Listen, my friend: Your God hasn't stopped talking, healing, intervening, or directing. He has not stopped loving you just as fiercely as He did on the day He first thought of you and saw the life He had planned for you. No, He's been whispering to your heart, drawing you closer, being miraculously present with you moment after moment. And He wants to awaken you to what it means to be filled with His Spirit.

I have a feeling you've picked up this book because you want more than ordinary. You want to experience God, hear from God, and know Him as a friend. You want the full relationship that is available to you, with nothing missing, and nothing short of all He has to offer. My prayer is that this book becomes more than words on a page, that it becomes a door for you to discover a deeper understanding of God, others, and yourself—awakening hope inside you, stirring life where you feel discouraged, and prompting you to pursue God in His fullness.

My prayer is that as you become more aware that the same Spirit of God who filled Jesus and raised Him from the dead is living inside you, it will be impossible for you to remain satisfied with anything less than His full presence. You'll look for the Holy Spirit in your everyday situations. You'll wake up listening for His voice. And you'll boldly do exactly what He asks because the risk of following Him is worth the reward of being used by Him.

I believe this book will change you. Not because of the words I write but because I believe God wants to meet you in the pages ahead. I believe He will invite you to shift your perception of what is natural and what is supernatural. And I believe you will be prompted to shift your expectation of what you and God can accomplish together through His miraculous intervention in your everyday life.

Your Invitation to a Deeper Relationship with God

Make no mistake, the Enemy of our hearts is terrified of what we might discover or be reminded of here. But the Spirit of truth, the Holy Spirit, is drawing us, as daughters of God, back into an understanding of Him in His fullness. He's removing doubt and confusion. He doesn't want to be crowded into a corner, welcome only in certain situations or during special church services.

The Holy Spirit wants us to know Him so He can make Jesus real to us. This is why He came. He wants *you* to know Him so Jesus can be real to *you*. And even now, He's preparing our hearts for what will come next.

I'll admit that I am still a student of His presence. I hold a degree in biblical studies, and I have been a friend of the Spirit for nearly thirty years. Yet daily He reveals a new understanding of who He is and who I am. That's because no matter how long we've known Him, there is more of Him for us to discover. There's a deeper relationship with God available both to you and to me.

So I invite you to join me. Let's sit and ask the Spirit to meet with us and teach us. Do you feel that stirring of expectation? Do you feel that heartbeat of hope? Let's talk about what it means to be awakened by the Spirit of God. Let's experience God So Close.

Let's Pray

Father God,

We start with love and gratitude. Thank You for loving us so much that You made a way for us to be together. Thank You for the gift of Your Son and the gift of Your Spirit. We want to know You, to be led by You, and to understand what it means to be full of Your presence. We believe You are exactly who You say You are and You will do everything You say You will do. Remove all confusion in our hearts and minds. Speak to us clearly. Our only aim is to know You more so we can love You and others more fully. Awaken our hearts to Your Spirit. Lead us in love. In Jesus' name we pray. Amen.

CHAPTER 1

THE INVITATION OF THE HOLY SPIRIT

God Wants You to Know Him

I was ten years old the first time I encountered the Spirit of God. Most of my friends were taking vacations to Disneyland or to the beach that summer, but my parents drove our family across the country because of what they'd heard was taking place in some church services on the East Coast. The reports were that God had come, and people's lives were being changed. My parents wanted our family to experience whatever that meant for us. So we packed up the minivan my momma earned selling Tupperware and drove for two days from Oklahoma City to Pensacola, Florida.

We were close to the beach, but we wouldn't see it that trip. We had come for one thing: we wanted to be in the church building where God had come in a unique way. We prayed the reports we'd heard were true.

When we arrived at the church, a line had formed outside well before the evening service had begun. People had camped out for hours, hoping to get into the sanctuary that night. Many had come farther than we had and were willing to do whatever it took to secure a seat inside. They, too, had heard the rumors and wanted to see for themselves what exactly was happening there.

As the doors opened and the line began to move forward, a living anticipation awoke within me. I sensed that something significant was about to happen. To this day, as I write about it, I remember the expectation I felt about what would take place that night.

We walked up the steps and through the tall doors of the church surrounded by hundreds of people, eager to find a seat. Ushers directed us toward an overflow section, but at the last moment we were told we could go into the main auditorium. When I close my eyes today, I can still see the thick jewel-toned carpet and the glowing sanctuary lights.

My family found a seat on the right side of the room. Worship music was playing and people were bustling. There was so much going on around me, but I sensed something else as well. I was still so young. I had been a Christian since I was five, but this was brand-new. No one had told me what I was supposed to experience, feel, think, or see. Yes, my parents had taught me well about who God was in Scripture. I knew all the stories, but I had never felt like this before. I wasn't just sensing the excitement of the people. In that moment, I was also aware of something supernatural in the unseen world around me. I truly believed that at any moment God Himself would walk into the room and I would see Him with my very own eyes.

What happened next marked my life. I couldn't tell you which songs were sung or the details of what the man at the podium spoke about that night. But I can tell you that when they extended an invitation for people to come to the front for prayer, I found my little feet walking down the aisle, with my daddy following behind me. In my heart I knew that God was going to meet with me in a way He hadn't before.

The front was crowded. It seemed as if most of the people had left their seats and made their way to the altar. Before I could walk even halfway down the aisle, a member of the prayer team came toward me. They were meeting people as they came because they knew there wouldn't be enough room for everyone at the front. I can't remember much about the woman who approached me or what she prayed except that as she came close, so did God.

Suddenly, everything about the room changed. It was like I wasn't even on earth. It felt like heaven. I closed my eyes and encountered God's perfect peace. In that moment I felt fully loved. It was both a physical and spiritual experience in which I felt as if Jesus Himself were standing in front of me. In my body, I felt the Holy Spirit rest on my heart like you might feel the warmth of a heated stove or the weight of a heavy blanket draped over your shoulders. In my spirit, the peace I experienced felt thick, like sweet honey on the inside, melting away all fear and uncertainty. My own legs couldn't hold me up in the weight of God's presence, so I dropped to the floor in worship.

I was in the presence of the Holy Spirit, and absolutely nothing else mattered.

That night was the first of many encounters with the Spirit of God. Over the course of that summer and the years that followed, I continued not only to feel God's presence but also to see miracles unfold in front of my eyes, incidents that defied science and logic and can only be described as supernatural. As a child, I saw God do wonderful works that still cause me to marvel at His awesome power. These events marked me. I became unsatisfied with just hearing about God. I wanted to meet with Him again and again, and I learned He wanted to keep meeting with me too.

I also learned another foundational truth that has given my faith solid ground throughout most of my life: Who God is today is exactly who He has always been. He created us to know Him, and through the sacrifice of Jesus and the gift of the Holy Spirit, we can be together with Him forever—beginning right now.

The Holy Spirit Changes Everything

Today I know much more about the Holy Spirit, whom I encountered that night all those years ago. While my experience was pure, the scriptural understanding I gained over the decades that followed made what I knew of God even more secure. I learned who the Holy Spirit revealed Himself to be in the Word. I learned how He moved throughout history and the early Church. And I learned what the Spirit's role is in the life of the Believer and the Church.

But that one encounter with God taught me something else. I learned that one moment in God's presence can do more to transform a person's life than a thousand moments simply hearing about Him. I am certain that when a person meets God and discovers He isn't just *out there* but is a real, loving friend who comes close and speaks directly to us, we become unsatisfied with simply talking about Him. Just as you might expect if you were to walk into a room and meet Jesus, when the Spirit of God is in the room, faith rises. Hope rushes in. Joy overflows. Peace rests. Strength comes. Determination ignites. When we meet the Spirit of the everlasting God, everything changes. Because He isn't just a feeling; He is God.

He is the same Spirit who helped create the world, who filled Jesus and raised Him from the dead, who moved through the apostles, and who worked miracles across the ages. He makes Jesus alive in us. As Believers in Jesus Christ, we have been given the gift of not only knowing the Holy Spirit but also being filled by Him. My hope is that as you read this book, you encounter Him for yourself.

How Well Do You Know the Holy Spirit?

So, my friend, I have to ask you a question: How well do you know the Holy Spirit? Be honest with yourself. I'm not talking about how much you know *about* Him. I'm asking, how well do you know the Holy Spirit as your friend? How clearly do you hear His voice? How real is He in your everyday life? How often do you follow His promptings? These might be new ideas you haven't previously considered, but God wants us to know Him and to reveal His power and love to the world around us. Few understand the depth of relationship He offers and the power He has given us.

The truth is, if the events that have unfolded in our lifetimes have taught us anything, it's that we must know God outside the four walls of the church. We must be able to follow the Holy Spirit as our guide and learn from Him even when we are not in the presence of a physical guide like a pastor or teacher. Long gone are the days of believing that the Holy Spirit of God only attends certain church services or speaks to or through certain people. As Believers, we are carriers of His Spirit and have been filled with His power and presence, and it's for His glory that we've been given gifts to impact the world and reveal the message of Jesus. We must know what it means for God to go with us wherever we go. We must learn to hear His voice and follow it, not just for the world out there but also for the sake of our own relationship with the Lord and for the people He has placed in our lives for a purpose.

Our Enemy's Mission

This is why the Enemy of our hearts works so hard to prevent us from learning about the kind of encounter and relationship with God available to us. Our Enemy knows that when we have the Holy Spirit within us and allow God to move through us, the kingdom of heaven invades the earth. When we are filled with the same Spirit who moved through Jesus, we become a threat to the kingdom of darkness. We aren't just knowers of God; we are His hands and feet, His mouth and His ears, carriers of His Spirit who are made in His likeness. We are children of the King who understand the authority we have and the power we possess.

The Enemy warns, "The Holy Spirit is strange. He can't be controlled. He's only for 'certain kinds' of Christians. What will nonbelievers think if they come to your church and see things they don't understand? How can you be sure you're not allowing some bad spirit into your life?"

Just as the Enemy spoke to and tempted Jesus in the desert, even quoting Scripture at times, he also tempts us by asking if we are sure about what God has said in His Word concerning His Spirit.

Our Enemy's mission is simple and intentional. If he can separate us from the power of God, then we will not be able to understand who we are as God's children. Make no mistake: the Enemy has not taken the power away from the Church; he merely attempts to convince the Church that we do not possess it.

I have witnessed beautiful churches full of wonderful people who treat God as someone who only did great and miraculous things in the past, not someone who does great and miraculous things *now*. So often we live as if we will only get to know God, experience closeness with Him, and see His wonders later on—when we reach heaven.

> Make no mistake: the Enemy has not taken the power away from the Church; he merely attempts to convince the Church that we do not possess it.

Yet He offers us the opportunity to know and experience Him today while we are still alive on earth.

That's part of why Jesus taught us to pray, "Our Father in heaven, hallowed be your name, your kingdom come, your will be done, on earth as it is in heaven" (Matthew 6:9–10). As this prayer goes on to talk about the weighty issues of forgiveness and temptation and sin, we might overlook the line "your kingdom come . . . on earth as it is in heaven." This prayer isn't about someday in the future. This is a prayer about the present that has remained the same across the ages. Jesus prompted us to speak to the Father about His will being carried out on earth *today*. God wants us to know Him and make Him known in *this* moment.

Your Eternal Life Has Already Begun

Friend, I don't know if you've already learned this or if you just need a reminder, but Jesus didn't give His life simply so we could spend eternity with Him after we die. The Father sent Jesus so we could become fully alive in Christ and be full of His power right now, while there is still breath in our lungs.

I wonder, why is it so easy for our Enemy to convince us that an infinite God would wait for our physical death before He gives us access to Himself? We often act as if, when we became Christians, God said to us, "Yep, I took care of that sin business for you. You're welcome. So I'll see you in approximately one hundred years. Hang on in this rough life until then, and I'll pick you up when you're done here."

That's not our Dad. Our Dad didn't leave us alone after Jesus returned to heaven. Jesus said to His friends in a story we will examine more closely in the chapters ahead: "I will ask the Father, and he will give you another advocate to help you and be with you forever—the Spirit of truth. The world cannot accept him, because it neither sees him nor knows him. But you know him, for he lives with you and will be in you. I will not leave you as orphans; I will come to you" (John 14:16–18).

He is available. His heart is turned toward us. And He is with us through His Holy Spirit today.

How does Jesus come to us? He sends the Spirit of truth! Sister, our Dad isn't away on business, distracted, or preoccupied with something else more important. He is the Dad who was there when we were born, reached out His arms as we took our first steps, and whispered to our hearts daily until they were drawn back to His. There hasn't been one moment of our lives when He has been turned away from us, and there will never be a moment going forward when He is unaware of our future. He is available. His heart is turned toward us. And He is with us through His Holy Spirit today. We can never forget that God has proven throughout history that His aim is for His children to be with Him. From Genesis to Revelation, the Bible tells this story of God's love for us and His desire to be our Father.

I don't know what your relationship with the Holy Spirit has been like in the past. I don't know what you've been taught or who you have known Him to be leading up to this moment. But He wants to meet you as He met me and millions of others. He doesn't want you to be enraptured by just one encounter. He wants to fill you and for you to be aware of His presence continually, every day of your life—each one a reminder of God's purposeful pursuit of your heart.

Our Deepest Longing

I believe this is the deep longing of our hearts: to know God as He intended us to know Him.

Yes, there are many things we crave in life. There are many things we believe will satisfy the insatiable seeking we all experience. We tend to think that if we only had a family who didn't struggle, a bigger and more affordable house, bills that are paid, health that is secure, a good job and clear mission and sense of accomplishment, then we'd finally feel fulfilled. But, while these are all good things, they will not satisfy our ultimate longing for joy and peace and hope. It is the Spirit of God we've been searching for all along. It's His presence that has been missing in our lives.

> This is the deep longing of our hearts: to know God as He intended us to know Him.

As the ancient worshiper said, "My soul yearns, even faints, for the courts of the LORD; my heart and my flesh cry out for the living God" (Psalm 84:2). Deep within us, we don't want to be people who just hear about God; we want to be people who believe everything He said is true. We want to know Him for ourselves. We want the living God to come, and we want to meet Him as one speaks with a friend face-to-face.

This is what He wants for us as well. God is inviting us, His daughters, to come discover His heart in a way we didn't know, or maybe had forgotten, was possible.

Perhaps it has been a while since you felt Him close. Perhaps you've never had a moment similar to what I described as a young girl. Maybe it's seemed as if the Holy Spirit has belonged to every Believer but you in a personal way. We are all on different parts of our journey, but I believe that if given the chance, you'd ask Him to come. And I believe that if you knew He was asking to meet with you, you'd accept His invitation.

Pioneering a Road of Relationship

What we are about to embark on in this book is no little journey. We are pioneering together a road of relationship with God that not everyone knows is available or chooses to accept. We are leaving behind what hasn't fueled us, what hasn't fed us, and the false boundaries where fear kept us from forging ahead with our Father, Friend, and Comforter.

But here's the thing: We cannot pioneer *and* take old roads. We cannot pioneer and go where everyone else has already gone, following the path they took to get there. The road before us is one outlined by Scripture, but often overlooked. So, if you choose to take this journey, we will have to cut through the overgrown places where lies are tangled with truth. We will have to cut through the confusion about who the Spirit of God is and what He makes available to us. We'll have to refocus our pursuit from *knowledge about* God to *intimacy with* Him. And we will reclaim territory from the Enemy, who wants to lure us away from a personal relationship with the Holy Spirit and distract us with empty practices and dry religion.

Pioneering by definition is not conventional. God's invitation to a full life with Him involves not conforming to this world but being transformed by the renewing of our minds through His Word and His Spirit (Romans 12:2). So let's ask Him to do just that. Let's ask the Holy Spirit to take what we thought we knew about Him and clarify it. Scripture plainly says, "The person without the Spirit does not accept the things that come from the Spirit of God but considers them foolishness, and cannot understand them because they are discerned only through the Spirit" (1 Corinthians 2:14).

> Let's ask the Holy Spirit to take what we thought we knew about Him and clarify it.

Let's ask the Holy Spirit to meet with us and explain to us spiritual things that foolish people cannot understand. Let's break free from believing the Enemy's lies about what God can't do. And let's go to His Word, looking at who the Holy Spirit reveals Himself to be and what our response to Him should look like. Let's bravely consider the power of a life awakened by the same Spirit who filled, led, and empowered Jesus while He walked the earth.

I believe that no matter how close God has been to you in

the past, there's a deeper, closer, and even more familiar experience available to you. No matter how much you know about Him, there's more to discover because He is infinite. There are no borders of the great expanse of God's being. And day by day, moment by moment, He is inviting you deeper into His heart.

Let's Pray

Father God,

We love You. Thank You for sending into our hearts Your Holy Spirit, who reveals the truth of who Jesus is and the love You have for us. Help us feel Your presence in the room with us even now. Bring us peace, hope, joy, and whatever else we need to be confident that You love us and are with us.

We believe that You have more for us to learn and experience. We trust You as You lead us deeper into Your heart through the revelation of Your Word. Mark this time in our lives as a season when we bravely began to follow You and discover the secrets of Your heart. May we be transformed by the power and presence of Your Holy Spirit. In Jesus' name we pray. Amen.

Let's Reflect

As we begin our journey into a deeper understanding of who the Holy Spirit is, let's take a moment to write down who we know Him to be today. When you complete this book, we'll revisit these same questions.

1. I've always thought of the Holy Spirit as . . .
2. When I think of the power God has given me, the first thing that comes to mind is . . .

Circle these True/False statements with your understanding today.

True or False   The Holy Spirit is a person.

True or False   The Holy Spirit speaks directly to Believers in Jesus today.

True or False   The Holy Spirit fills Believers in Jesus today, supplying supernatural power and wisdom.

True or False   The Holy Spirit gives spiritual gifts to Believers in Jesus today.

CHAPTER 2

THE PROMISE OF THE FATHER

Who Is the Holy Spirit?

It was my third year of college, and I had just transferred to another private Christian university closer to home. Jared and I had been married for a year, and as a twenty-something married woman who had basically completed her degree in biblical studies, I felt there wasn't much left to learn. (Ha! Now, doesn't that tell you how little I actually knew!)

I was enrolled in a class called The Person and Work of the Holy Spirit, which seemed like a refresher course, and I welcomed the idea of an easy class in my junior year of college. After all, I already knew so much about the Trinity from all my other studies.

By Trinity, I mean that I understood there is one true God—Father, Son, and Holy Spirit (or Holy Ghost, as some denominations call Him). I'd taken classes that had explained that the three persons of the Trinity are all God, because they are called God in Scripture:

- God the Father is called "God" in 1 Corinthians 8:6: "There is but one God, the Father, from whom all things came and for whom we live."
- The Son, Jesus, is called "God" in Matthew 1:23: "'The virgin will conceive and give birth to a son, and they will call him Immanuel' (which means 'God with us')."
- The Holy Spirit is called "the Lord" (meaning "God") in 2 Corinthians 3:17: "Now the Lord is the Spirit, and where the Spirit of the Lord is, there is freedom."

I also knew that while Scripture calls each of the three persons of the Trinity "God," it also reminds us that they are one.

- Deuteronomy 6:4 says, "Hear, O Israel: The LORD our God, the LORD is one."
- Jesus said in John 10:30, "I and the Father are one."
- First Timothy 2:5 says, "There is one God and one Mediator who can reconcile God and humanity—the man Christ Jesus" (NLT).

When it came to the Holy Spirit, I was secure in what I knew as well. After all, I had met the Holy Spirit for myself when I was young, remember? I thought this class would be a breeze, and the professor might as well just give me an A and save us both the time.

On the first day of the course, I stepped into the classroom, found my seat, and listened to the professor's welcome. I picked up a syllabus as a stack of them circulated the room and skimmed over the plan for the semester. *What will the professor be teaching my classmates?* I wondered. I wasn't paying full attention as he began his introduction, but something he said snapped my mind right back into the room.

We were instructed to make sure that when we turned in our assignments, we capitalized the Holy Spirit's name and referred to the Holy Spirit as *He* rather than *It*. The professor wanted us to know from day one that the Holy Spirit is very much a person. He is God, and He deserves the same honor and respect as the Father and the Son.

I wish someone had taken a picture of my expression the moment I realized that after three years of Bible school, a lifetime of growing up in the Church, and even my own personal encounters with the Holy Spirit, I had not really thought of Him as a person. I knew He was God, but back then I was still most comfortable calling the Holy Spirit an *it*.

If someone had asked me, "Who is the Holy Spirit?" I would have answered, "It's the Spirit of God." I don't think I am alone either. I mean, after all, the Greek word used for "Spirit" in the New Testament, *pneuma*, means "breath, wind, or spirit."[1] The Holy Spirit doesn't have a body. So what leads us to believe that He is a person?

I'll answer that question with another question. Are you your body? I know it's weird. Follow me for a minute. You are a person. That is a fact. But are you your body, or do you simply possess a body? If something happened to a part of your body, would you stop being you? The answer is easily no, because we are not our bodies. We are spirits who live in bodies and have minds and emotions. As a matter of fact, when you die, your body will remain on earth, but your spirit will receive a new body in heaven. Why? Because your spirit is who you really are.

In the same way, the Holy Spirit is a person without a body. He's not an *it* or some impersonal wind or force. He is the Spirit of God. If Jesus was God *in the flesh*—100 percent God and 100 percent man—then the Holy Spirit is 100 percent God *without flesh*.

The Holy Spirit possesses all the attributes of personhood—a mind, will, and emotions—but He doesn't have the confines of skin to keep Him in one place. Jesus and Scripture make the personhood of the Holy Spirit clear. Let's see what they say.

A Helper Who Abides with Us Forever

As Jesus and His friends gathered in an upper room to share a final meal before He went to the cross, He gave one last teaching to the disciples. These men had traveled with Jesus for three years. They had seen His works, participated in His miracles, and listened to His words. But on this night, Jesus told them He would be going to His Father, and they could not follow Him right away. Having given so much of their lives to following Him, the disciples were concerned why they couldn't come with Him. I can only imagine the human response that rose in their hearts: *What does He mean? What are we supposed to do? What will happen to us when He leaves?*

However, knowing that they would need support after He returned to His Father, Jesus explained who was coming to help: "I will pray the Father, and He will give you another Helper, that He may abide with you forever—the Spirit of truth, whom the world cannot receive, because it neither sees Him nor knows Him; but you know Him, for He dwells with you and will be in you" (John 14:16–17 NKJV).

This specific description of the Holy Spirit is important, and each part reveals the truth about who He is.

"Another Helper"

The meaning of the Greek word translated as "another" is "another of the same kind."[2] It's not as if Jesus said, "I'm going away, but I'm sending this completely different thing to be with you." No, the translation means "another like Himself."[3]

If there can be no disunity among the Father, Son, and Holy Spirit and they eternally remain perfectly one, then the Spirit must be like Jesus. And we know who Jesus is. The Spirit feels like Jesus. He speaks like Jesus. He comforts like Jesus. And He loves like Jesus.

"Abide with You Forever"

Jesus didn't say the Holy Spirit would come and stay with them awhile. Jesus said the Holy Spirit would come and abide with them forever. This is the same Spirit the Old Testament prophet Joel prophesied about hundreds of years earlier. Speaking on behalf of God, Joel said, "It shall come to pass afterward that I will pour out My Spirit on all flesh" (2:28 NKJV). While the Holy Spirit had been present on earth in specific ways before Jesus came, it was not until Jesus returned to heaven and the Father poured out the Spirit that the Spirit came to remain on earth.

"You Know Him, for He Dwells with You"

Jesus made it clear to His friends that they had already met this Helper through Him. They had gotten to know the Holy Spirit through Jesus' life and ministry. As they had become familiar with Jesus, they had also become familiar with the Holy Spirit, who had dwelled with them in Jesus.

"Will Be in You"

This is my favorite part of what Jesus said about the Holy Spirit because it's so clear. Jesus said the Holy Spirit not only had been *with* them but also would be *in* them. If you think my face was astonished as I learned the Holy Spirit is a person, imagine the faces of Jesus' friends as He explained to them that the same Spirit who moved through Him would *be in them*. Can you picture those glances darting around to one another? *Did He just say the Spirit would be in* us?

But Jesus' foretelling of the Holy Spirit is not the only time the Spirit's personhood was revealed.

The Person and Work of the Holy Spirit

Throughout Scripture, we see evidence of the person and work of the Holy Spirit. For example, the Holy Spirit has a mind, will, and emotions. He also acts as a person who is not confined to a body.

The Holy Spirit Has a Mind

First Corinthians 2:10–11 teaches us that the Holy Spirit has a mind: "The Spirit searches all things, even the deep things of God. For who knows a person's thoughts except their own spirit within them? In the same way no one knows the thoughts of God except the Spirit of God." Just as you know your own thoughts, the Holy Spirit knows God's thoughts because He is God. It's clear that the Holy Spirit is a person who thinks.

The Holy Spirit Has a Will

Scripture also tells us the Holy Spirit can make decisions and possesses a will. First Corinthians 12:4–11 lists the Spirit's various gifts, then says, "All these are the work of one and the same Spirit, and he distributes them to each one, just as he determines." The Holy Spirit knows best, and He acts according to what He wills, distributing each spiritual gift to Believers as He chooses.

The Holy Spirit Has Emotions

In addition to a mind and will, the Holy Spirit also possesses emotions. For example, He can be grieved. Ephesians 4:30–32 says, "Do not grieve the Holy Spirit of God, with whom you were sealed for the day of redemption. Get rid of all bitterness, rage and anger, brawling and slander, along with every form of malice. Be kind and compassionate to one another, forgiving each other, just as in Christ God forgave you."

Can I remind you of something you already know? The force of gravity doesn't have emotions. The force of wind responding to the changing temperatures of the earth cannot be grieved. Only a being who possesses feelings and emotions can be grieved or made sorrowful. This shouldn't shock us because, once again, the Holy Spirit is God, as are the Father and Son, who also possess emotions. Jesus wept over the loss of His friend Lazarus (John 11:35). God's anger is mentioned repeatedly throughout Scripture. The Holy Spirit is no different.

> The force of gravity doesn't have emotions. The force of wind responding to the changing temperatures of the earth cannot be grieved. Only a being who possesses feelings and emotions can be grieved or made sorrowful.

The Holy Spirit Acts as a Person

In addition to having thoughts, making decisions, and experiencing feelings, the Holy Spirit also acts as a person. For example, the Holy Spirit teaches and reminds us of truth. Jesus said, "All this I have spoken while still with you. But the Advocate, the Holy Spirit, whom the Father will send in my name, *will teach* you all things and *will remind* you of everything I have said to you" (John 14:25–26).

The Holy Spirit also testifies, giving evidence of Jesus and the works He has done on the earth. In John 15:26, Jesus said, "When the Advocate comes, whom I will send to you from the Father—the Spirit of truth who goes out from the Father—he *will testify* about me." This is super important because everything that the Holy Spirit does reveals the truth of who Jesus is.

The Holy Spirit helps us pray. Paul reminded the Roman church, "The Spirit helps us in our weakness. We do not know what we ought to pray for, but the Spirit himself *intercedes* for us through wordless groans" (Romans 8:26).

Jesus told His friends in John 16:13 that the Holy Spirit guides and speaks: "When he, the Spirit of truth, comes, he *will guide you* into all the truth. He will not speak on his own; he *will speak* only what he hears, and he will tell you what is yet to come."

The Holy Spirit Is Not Confined to a Body

The Holy Spirit is a person, just as real as Jesus. But because the Holy Spirit is not confined to a body, Jesus said something remarkable to His friends during their final meal together: "It is to your advantage that I go away; for if I do not go away, the Helper will not come to you; but if I depart, I will send Him to you" (John 16:7 NKJV).

How could it possibly be better for the disciples for Jesus to leave? From Jesus' conception to His resurrection, the Holy Spirit was a part of Jesus' life and ministry on the earth. Once Jesus completed His work on earth and returned to the Father in heaven, the Spirit would come and fill all Believers, just as

He had filled Jesus. Jesus said this was how He'd continue to be with His followers "always, to the very end of the age" (Matthew 28:20).

The Holy Spirit wouldn't be present in only one room at a time, as Jesus was. Instead, He would fill the sons and daughters of God just as God had promised through Joel. The Holy Spirit wouldn't just be all around them; He would be *within* them! And as Believers in Jesus, this is what you and I get to experience today.

The Holy Spirit—God Within Us

I feel like that was a lot to take in, so let's recap. The Father sent the gift of the Spirit for all Believers, and, like the disciples, you and I can know Him personally. Jesus is *God with us*. The Holy Spirit is *God within us*. The Holy Spirit does not have a body, but He's not an impersonal force. He has thoughts. He has feelings. He makes decisions. He teaches, speaks, comforts, and convicts.

The Holy Spirit of God makes Jesus alive in our hearts, and He wants us to have a real relationship with Him. He invites us to learn to hear His voice as He still speaks to us today. He invites us to follow His leading because He wants to be a part of our everyday lives. And He invites us to be filled with His power and share the good news of Jesus throughout the earth. He is the holy God who comes close.

But how do we interact with Him? And what does it mean to be filled by Him? We will discuss all this and more in the chapters ahead.

Let's Pray

Father God,

Some of us have heard from friends and family and pastors and books about who people say You are. And some of us haven't heard much about Your Spirit at all. But we want to know with confidence now that You've revealed Your Spirit to us and that You're telling us as a friend what we need to know about You. Help us open our Bibles and search for where Your Spirit shows up in Scripture. Help us read Your Word, listening for Your voice to show us what we didn't see or notice before. We believe the Holy Spirit has been poured out, so we ask You to reveal the person and work of the Spirit in our lives today. We pursue more than information about You. We pursue Your presence, God. We pause right here in this moment to make space for Your Spirit to do whatever He wants, trusting that He will make us like Jesus. Thank You for coming close to us. In Jesus' name we pray. Amen.

Let's Reflect

1. I think there is confusion in the Church surrounding the Holy Spirit because . . .
2. When it comes to the personhood of the Holy Spirit, I want to better understand . . .

CHAPTER 3

THE BREATH OF GOD

God Is as Close as Your Breath

I was somewhere around thirty weeks pregnant with my first child, Kolton, when I began to experience preterm labor. Continual contractions, which had begun as simple reflexes by my body to practice for birth, had become something far more serious. Thankfully I had already been referred to a perinatologist for a few underlying conditions, and I trusted that this doctor trained to treat high-risk pregnancies was well prepared to help me handle this new complication.

During my appointment the doctor and I discussed what would need to be done to stop the contractions as well as to prepare for the baby's arrival just in case our efforts to hold off labor were unsuccessful. One part of my doctor's plan involved a series of steroid shots, which would help Kolton's lungs mature. My baby hadn't yet come into the world, but the doctors were already focused on his first breath.

When Kolton was born just a few weeks later, I listened for that first gasp of air and the cry that followed. As his newborn noises filled the hospital room and the nurses confirmed that all was well, I was so grateful that everything was just as it should be.

As a mom I remember all my children's first breaths. Those first piercing cries announcing, "New life is here," were beautiful to me. But you know, while I hold closely the memories of those first moments of my children's lives, I wonder how much more God thinks about the first breaths His children took.

When Eve took her first breath, God was with her. Before Eve met another human, she knew only the holy, living God. How do we know this? Genesis 2:22 describes how God formed Eve and *then* brought her to Adam. I love thinking about the time Eve was entirely alone with the Lord. She must have felt absolute peace, total security, and complete trust. She knew only the goodness of the Lord.

From the beginning of creation, God has been present with His children, as close as their very breath.

A beautiful picture, this moment teaches us an important truth: from the beginning of creation, God has been present with His children, as close as their very breath.

The Breath of God in Creation

To be honest, there was a time when I would open my Bible and read the story of how God created the world and I imagined Him far away. I pictured Him standing in heaven speaking down toward earth, calling from the other side of the universe. And when I imagined the creation story that way, God seemed distant from the beginning of all things—as though everything He did was from afar. But I think if we read the creation story again, we might see how His Spirit was woven into everything He made, specifically us.

Genesis 1:1–2 says, "In the beginning God created the heavens and the earth. Now the earth was formless and empty, darkness was over the surface of the deep, and the Spirit of God was hovering over the waters." I love that image of the Spirit of God hovering. The Hebrew word for "Spirit" used in this passage is *ruach*, or רוּחַ, and it means "spirit, breath, wind."[1] Imagine God's Spirit, like breath, exhaling over the surface of the waters.

It was from this nearness that He spoke, "Let there be light" (v. 3), and light was. He continued to speak and created planets and stars, land and seas, and animals and birds. And then when it was time to make us, God said: "Let us make mankind in our image, in our likeness" (v. 26).

Pause for just a second. Notice God didn't say, "Let *Me* make mankind in *My* image." The Father, Son, and Holy Spirit made the decision together to create humankind. Genesis records, "Then the LORD God formed a man from the dust of the ground and *breathed into his nostrils the breath of life*, and the man became a living being" (2:7).

I'm a big fan of highlighting books and making notes. If I could tuck a pen into your hand, I'd say, "Underline that part about God breathing into man's nostrils the breath of life." Why? Because this is foundational truth. From the moment we were created and God breathed His Spirit into us, He has been as close as our breath. Take a deep breath in, friend . . . He is that close.

I want to offer a deeper teaching here. It's a story I believe will change how you think about the breath in your lungs.

The Breath of God in His Name

In Exodus, we meet a man named Moses. I never like to assume what people know about the Bible, so I'll tell you a bit of his story as though you don't already know it.

Moses was chosen by God to lead the Israelites, God's people, out of bondage. The Israelites had been slaves in Egypt for more than four hundred years, and God told Moses their deliverance would come with his help. While speaking with the Lord, Moses asked for reassurance that God would help them. And the Lord answered, "Now you will see what I will do to Pharaoh: Because of my mighty hand he will let them go; because of my mighty hand he will drive them out of his country. . . . I am the LORD" (Exodus 6:1–2).

When we read "the LORD" here and in other parts of the Old Testament, the word in Hebrew is יהוה and transliterates to YHWH. This is the name of God that He revealed to Moses and that His people used across generations. And it is a name so sacred that even today many Jews do not write it or speak it. However, if you were going to try to pronounce it, all you would have to do is breathe in and out.

Wait . . . what does that mean?

Follow me here for just a second. You might have heard the name *Yahweh*. This is the same as YHWH but with vowel sounds added. The original Hebrew did not have vowel letters. Try pronouncing YHWH without any vowel sounds. Just begin forming the sound for the letter *Y*, then link it with the sound *H* makes. Remember, you're not saying *Yah*, *Yeh*, or *Yuh*. You're just piecing the individual letter sounds together. Do the same for the *H*, *W*, and the second *H*. Take just a second and actually try it.

Okay, what's the point? Here's something pretty remarkable. Many Jews will not write or speak the name YHWH because they believe it to be so holy. But for years, scholars have also discussed another possible reason it is hard to pronounce this name. I've heard it again and again over my years of study that the name God revealed to Moses cannot be pronounced because it is the sound of breath. To speak the name YHWH is to inhale and exhale.

Can we acknowledge how significant this is? When God formed Eve and breathed His Spirit into her, she came alive physically and spiritually. The moment she took her first breath, she declared the name of God. This is the name you spoke when you took your first breath as well. When I say that God is as close as our very breath, I don't simply mean that the idea of Him is close. I mean that, just as Scripture tells us, God "himself gives everyone life and breath and everything else" (Acts 17:25). And every breath of our lives declares His name.

The Breath of God Is Close to Us

I have to ask you, when you think of God right now, in this moment, where is He? Really pause and consider your answer. Do you imagine Him in heaven? Or do you think of Him there with you in the room?

I suppose it's not really a fair question because you and I both have likely heard that He is everywhere at once. Theologians call this aspect of God's nature *omnipresence*. Through the prophet Jeremiah, God said, "Do not I fill heaven and earth?" (Jeremiah 23:24).

But if you're like me, there are times when God seems closer than others. There are times when God seems so near that I understand what the psalmist David meant when he said, "Where can I go from your Spirit? Where can I flee from your presence?" (Psalm 139:7). In those seasons, God seems like a constant friend, truly "an ever-present help in trouble" (Psalm 46:1). Yet there are other times when it feels as if He is far away, busy helping everyone else but me. In those moments, I wonder, *Why does God seem so distant? Where is He?* I'm sure you've experienced similar feelings.

The reality is, no matter how we feel and no matter the season or situation, God is constantly close all the time. And more than that, He's always listening for His children. He spoke about the nation of Israel, His chosen people, saying, "Before they call I will answer; while they are still speaking I will hear" (Isaiah 65:24). This reveals the heart of God toward us, His children.

You might feel as if He isn't listening to your prayers. You might feel as if He doesn't care to respond to you. But our feelings don't change what is true about God. We have an attentive God who is continually with us, who listens for us as a parent listens for the cry of his child and responds.

> We have an attentive God who is continually with us, who listens for us as a parent listens for the cry of his child and responds.

Here's the thing though: just because God is near does not mean that we choose to interact with Him. I bet you know what I mean.

I'm a mom, and one thing moms know for certain is that just because a mom is in the room does not mean her children are paying attention to her. She can walk into a space, give a simple instruction, and her kids can be oblivious that she is even there unless they need something from her. And then, suddenly, she is *very* important. Do I need to complete this illustration, or did you already make the connection for yourself?

The truth is, while we have constant access to God because He is always near and paying attention to us, most of the time we don't choose to interact with Him. And I must ask, Why? If the Spirit of the living God is in the room with us, as close as our breath, then why don't we act like it?

Two Reasons We Overlook the Holy Spirit

Here's what I think: I believe we often unintentionally overlook God's Spirit for one of two reasons. We're either so familiar with Him that we forget about Him while we're focused on everything else in our lives, or we overlook Him because we don't fully understand who is in the room with us.

There are two women in the Bible who had similar encounters with God, and I believe by looking at their stories, we'll be encouraged to turn our hearts toward the Holy Spirit—to God in the room.

Martha—Familiarity Leads to Forgetfulness

Martha was a friend of Jesus and was known for her hospitality. Along with her sister, Mary, and her brother, Lazarus, she opened her home to Jesus and His friends during His travels. She loved the Lord, and she served her guests with honor and attended to all their needs.

Once while hosting Jesus and His disciples, Mary sat and listened to Jesus, leaving Martha with the responsibility to serve Jesus and the rest of her guests. Frustrated, Martha asked the Lord to direct Mary to help her.

Jesus answered, "Martha, Martha . . . you are worried and

upset about many things, but few things are needed—or indeed only one" (Luke 10:41–42). Jesus told Martha that her sister had chosen the better option and it would not be taken away from her.

I wonder how those words landed in Martha's heart. She had been consumed by the process of loving Jesus well by serving Him. Yet she had overlooked the gift of God's presence with her. She had forgotten that God Himself, in the person of Jesus, was in her house!

I wonder if she had this attitude toward Jesus because He was so familiar to her. Scripture tells us that Martha's family was loved by Jesus. Yes, Jesus loves everyone, but Jesus had a close friendship with this family while He was on earth. When Martha's brother, Lazarus, died, Scripture tells us that "Jesus wept" (John 11:35). His disciples even noted how much Jesus loved Lazarus (v. 36).

I wonder if it was because of Martha's familiarity with Jesus that she was able to treat His visit to her house that day as if it were any other day with Him.

Does this sound like anyone else you know? I'm not talking about serving over sitting. I'm talking about knowing that God is always with us and forgetting the significance of that because His presence is constant.

So what is the better way? What is the one thing needed that Jesus offered Martha? God offers His presence as a gift, filling our hearts with His living breath, just as air fills our lungs.

The Samaritan Woman—Not Realizing Who Is with You

The other reason we often unintentionally overlook the Holy Spirit is because we do not fully perceive the importance of who is in the room with us. Yes, many of us know much about God, but even though He is close, we don't recognize His presence. There was another woman in Scripture, this one without a name, who knew much about God but didn't recognize Him when He spoke to her face-to-face.

We know her as the Samaritan woman and, based on her interaction with Jesus, we know that she had great wisdom about who God was. Even though she was a woman, who wouldn't have been taught as the men were taught at that time, and even though she was a Samaritan, a group that had split from God's people generations earlier, she still knew that God was sending a Savior for His people. She knew the Messiah would teach them all things.

Yet even with all this information, she lacked spiritual understanding of who this Savior would be, and she didn't recognize Him when He stood in front of her. Like us, she had a lot of knowledge about who God was, but she didn't recognize Him when He came close. It took Jesus saying, "I, the one speaking to you—I am he" for her life to be changed (John 4:26).

Are You Aware of God in the Room with You?

From the encounters of both these women, we see that it is possible to stand in the presence of God and carry on as if we were not. These weren't bad women. These weren't women who should feel any shame for what they did or how they interacted with Jesus. They were just like us.

We carry on with what must be done in life because we are busy ladies. And while we are grateful for God's presence, there are other things that require our attention. We have learned what His Word says, and we know we have a Messiah. But we have forgotten that just because God is always present does not mean that He should be ignored. And just because He is with us does not mean we automatically recognize the God who is in the room.

I believe if Jesus were to come to dinner tonight at your house, you wouldn't spend the evening in the kitchen like Martha. I believe if Jesus were to knock on your office door or open the passenger door of your car and climb in, you wouldn't shrug your shoulders and go about your day. Jesus? *He'd* get our attention.

But here's the thing: Scripture tells us that Jesus is seated at the right hand of the Father (Ephesians 1:20). He will come to earth again in the last days to judge both the living and the dead (2 Timothy 4:1), but for now He sits in heaven. That is the position of Jesus the Son of God. So who comes close to us?

The Holy Spirit is God in the room with you right now. But because He's invisible to our physical eyes, He is easily overlooked.

Scripture is clear: God's work continues on earth through the Holy Spirit, whom Jesus has sent. When we ask God to comfort us when we are sad, it's the Holy Spirit who comes close. When we need wisdom spoken to our hearts, it's the Holy Spirit who guides. When we read Scripture, it's the Holy Spirit who teaches us what God is really saying. The Holy Spirit is God in the room with you right now. But because He's invisible to our physical eyes, He is easily overlooked.

Jesus, we know. We understand Him. Jesus was fully God and fully man, and when He came to earth, He gave us someone to picture when we think of God. But the Holy Spirit? How do we speak to the Spirit? How do we get to know the Spirit? How do we interact with the Spirit? We know He is as close as our breath, but who is He really?

I believe if we *really* understood that the Holy Spirit is the Spirit of the one true Holy God, the same Spirit who filled Jesus and who reveals Jesus to us today, we would not be satisfied simply knowing He's around. We'd long to listen when He speaks, spend time getting to know Him, and want to go on adventures together, trusting that through Him we will know Christ better and become more like Him. The good news is that He's not just the God in the room. He's the God who fills us and is closer than our breath.

Let's Pray

Father God,

Thank You for being as close as our breath. I ask that the wind of Your presence as the breath of God would blow away all confusion and fear. Like a whirlwind, sweep through our hearts and stir up hope. Breathe life into the dead and dry places within us that have felt disconnected from You. Help us remember the wonder of simply being in the room with You. Fill us again with Your love. In Jesus' name we pray. Amen.

Let's Reflect

1. Why would you say it is important to remember that God is always with us?

2. In your own words, why do you think a person might overlook the presence of the Holy Spirit in the room? Do you tend to overlook the presence of the Holy Spirit in the room with you?

CHAPTER 4

THE HOLINESS OF GOD

Why the Wrath of God Matters

My teal green Bible was flipped open to Exodus. My mom and I were reading chapter by chapter through the Scriptures together, and as a nine-year-old I loved everything about it. I enjoyed spending time with my mom. I enjoyed checking off the small squares in the back of the Bible that showed I had completed the daily reading passage. But most of all, I loved learning about who God showed Himself to be in the lives of those who lived before me.

One particular day my mom and I sat down to read Exodus chapter 32. In the days leading up to it, my mom and I had read all about God leading the Israelites out of Egypt and the miraculous works surrounding their deliverance. We had read about the plagues in Egypt, God parting the waters, and the Egyptian army chasing the Israelites. It was all so exciting! Chapter 32 continued the story of the Israelites' journey to worship God in freedom.

As my mom and I took turns reading, I learned about Moses going up Mount Sinai, the mountain of God, to receive instructions from the Lord, and the Israelites growing impatient below. While they had seen miraculous works and experienced God's powerful deliverance, when Moses took a little longer than expected on the mountain, the Israelites believed God and Moses had abandoned them. So they formed an idol to worship instead of God.

God wasn't happy. He said to Moses, "I have seen this

people, and indeed it is a stiff-necked people! Now therefore, let Me alone, that My wrath may burn hot against them and I may consume them. And I will make of you a great nation" (Exodus 32:9–10 NKJV).

As an elementary-aged girl who had experienced the sweet presence of the Holy Spirit already, I found it a little confusing to read the words God spoke to Moses. Wrath didn't seem to be God's primary emotion when I spent time with Him. Consuming His people didn't seem like something my God would do in these modern times. I had so many questions, and fortunately I had a momma with the answers.

Perhaps you have questions when it comes to God's judgment or wrath too. Big ones that seem too daunting to even ask. But I have really good news. The wrath of God isn't proof that He is unloving. It is actually evidence of His pure goodness. And in the pages ahead we will examine why the wrath of God matters and how it impacts our understanding of the Holy Spirit.

I know you may be bracing yourself at this point. Maybe it sounds like it's about to get real uncomfortable real fast. I get it—a discussion like this isn't usually found in books like mine. Yet I fully believe this subject is important for us to understand so everything else is read with the correct perspective. So let's talk about God's holiness and His wrath.

I asked my editor if we could use emojis in this book. She said no. But I feel like sometimes, when used properly, emojis help convey tone that is otherwise missing in text. If I could use one, I would insert that little *eek!* face—the one with teeth that says, *Yikes! Not good*. This is the perfect spot for that expression because holiness and wrath are not topics that seem at first to draw us closer to God, right? They seem like topics that make us want to see if there's anything better in the chapters ahead. (Don't peek, but chapters 11 and 12 are two of my favorites.)

The thing is, to understand the presence of the Holy Spirit, we must understand not just that God is Spirit but also that He is holy. And to understand God's holiness, we have to discuss His wrath as well. But here's what I want you to know: I actually believe this chapter will draw you closer to Him. I'm not kidding. It will help you appreciate even more deeply why Jesus came for you. It will help you hold the reverence for the Holy Spirit that He is worthy of. And it will help you answer some hard questions about God and the world.

So grab your hiking stick (I own exactly zero of those because I don't hike), and let's look at this subject from a new vantage point.

What Is the Holiness of God?

Most of us begin our understanding of God and His love for us through the story of Jesus. Would you agree? At church, children sing songs about Jesus' love. They make crafts and hear stories about Jesus' love. It's not often that children are first taught they are sinful beings who need a Savior to rescue them from hell. No, we usually begin with love: "For God so loved the world that he gave his one and only Son, that whoever believes in him shall not perish but have eternal life" (John 3:16). Adults often hear of the sacrifice of Jesus in conjunction with their need for a Savior, and children learn songs like "Jesus Loves Me."

We learn about Jesus' birth and the cross and the empty

tomb. We focus on Christmas and Easter, and it's through this lens of a kind, loving, and gracious Jesus, who was fully God and fully man, dying to pay the debt we couldn't, that we view everything else we know of God. As a result, we easily skip over the fact that our kind, loving, gracious God is also an all-consuming fire. He is perfectly holy. He is entirely set apart from all that is evil, and nothing unholy can stand in His presence.

Yes, we may eventually learn these details, but I wonder how fully? How much do we allow the holiness of God to play a part in our worship of Him?

Let's take a close look at what *holiness* really means. As with any word, when you read the word *holy*, your personal experiences and previous understanding have already defined it for you. Perhaps you think of the reverence found in a large cathedral. Or maybe you think of the Holy Bible. When we talk about the holiness of God, it's important for us to fully understand how Scripture defines it.

The first use of a word meaning "holy" in Scripture is found in Genesis 2:3, which says, "God blessed the seventh day and made it *holy*, because on it God rested from all his work that he had done in creation" (ESV). The Hebrew word used here is *qadash*. It basically means "to be set apart or consecrated."[1] God separated the seventh day from the others and made it holy.

Similar to *qadash*, the Hebrew word we see used for God's holiness in the Bible is *qadosh*. See that one little difference in vowel sounds? Found in Isaiah 6:3, *qadosh* shows how the angels in heaven cry back and forth to one another, "*Holy, holy, holy* is the LORD of hosts; the whole earth is full of His glory!" (NKJV). *Qadosh* plainly means "holy or sacred."[2] Sometimes looking at the definition of an original word gives us further insight into what that word truly means. In this case, the word *qadosh* doesn't give us any additional understanding. But here's what we need to remember: Holiness isn't just on a list of things that define God. Holiness is part of His very identity. God is holy. Period.

> Holiness isn't just on a list of things that define God. Holiness is part of His very identity. God is holy. Period.

He gives us the best understanding of the word *holy* in His very nature. He is set apart from all that is evil. Psalm 113:5 declares, "Who is like the LORD our God, the One who sits enthroned on high?" No one! He alone is holy.

Why Does God's Holiness Matter?

I feel like I can hear you saying, "Becky, thank you, but I've got things to do . . . so can you please get to the point and tell me what this has to do with us? Why does understanding God's holiness matter?"

Since the beginning of time, God's perfect goodness and separateness from all that is evil affects how we interact with Him. God's holiness has always and will always shape His relationship with His children, including you. Here's how.

In the beginning Adam and Eve were perfectly like God. Everything they knew came from the perfect world into which they were placed. God could look at them and see His own goodness reflected. Everything Adam and Eve did was holy because they were set apart from all that was evil.

However, the serpent in the garden tempted Eve and prompted her to eat from the Tree of Knowledge of Good and

Evil. If she ate from it, she would no longer *only* have knowledge of what was good. She'd have knowledge of *both* good *and* evil. She would no longer be separated from all that was evil. When she ate from the tree, her eyes would be opened and her holiness would break. In that moment, when Adam and Eve disobeyed God and ate the forbidden fruit, they became unlike God. They became unholy.

I'm not saying the fruit transformed Adam and Eve into different beings as you might imagine happening in a movie (even though something must have changed about the way they looked because they felt the need to cover themselves). I am saying they were no longer perfectly like God, separate from all that was evil. This is where life as we know it was changed forever.

The relationship between God and humanity shifted. Now only God was separate from evil, and this meant that He must be separate from the children He created to love. Sin caused a distance that was never supposed to be there, but the Father, Son, and Holy Spirit had a plan in place to restore the relationship between God and man.

God knew what this separation meant. It didn't only mean distance. It meant that the all-consuming wrath of God that falls on everything that is unholy would now fall on His children.

A Simple Illustration of God's Wrath

When I explain sin and God's wrath to my three elementary-aged kids, I make it really simple. My illustration isn't perfect, but I'd like to share it with you because I think it might be helpful. Try not to laugh.

I explain to my kids that God is like a big bubble of perfect goodness. His bubble is called "holiness," and the only things allowed inside the bubble are things perfectly good like Him. Outside the bubble, God's judgment, anger, and fire consumes everything. It's because God is so good and loving that His justice destroys everything that is not.

For my children, I explain that when Adam and Eve sinned, they couldn't stay in the bubble because only perfect people like God could be with Him. When they disobeyed God, they immediately were outside the bubble, and everyone after Adam and Eve was born outside the bubble of God's holiness too.

But then I point to Jesus.

We had no way to find our way back into the protection of God's bubble on our own. We could never do enough, earn enough, or try hard enough to get back under the protection of His holiness. And outside the bubble was only sadness and pain and death. He didn't want it to be this way, but because we separated ourselves from Him, His wrath was on all of us!

So God sent Jesus to take all the wrath on Himself, like a superhero able to walk into the world that was unholy without becoming unholy. Then, when He died and rose again, His blood covered those of us who believe in Him, protecting us from the wrath of God. He made a door for us to enter the place that our sin had kept us from entering. Now when God looks at us, He sees the covering of His Son, Jesus, and we are spared.

While that is a highly limited illustration, it reminds us of an important truth. Even though we are still unholy, far from being perfect as He is perfect, we can come near to God because Jesus paid the penalty for our sin and covers us. "God made him who

Sin is anything that separates us from Him. And as a result of sin, we cannot be in the presence of a holy God without something—Someone— standing between us.

had no sin to be sin for us, so that in him we might become the righteousness of God" (2 Corinthians 5:21). "There is one God and one mediator between God and mankind, the man Christ Jesus" (1 Timothy 2:5).

You know, we often think of sin as something really "bad," but sin is anything that is unlike God. Sin is anything that separates us from Him. And as a result of sin, we cannot be in the presence of a holy God without something—Someone—standing between us.

How Can God Be Loving and Pour Out His Wrath?

In John 3:36 Jesus explained to us, "Whoever believes in the Son has eternal life, but whoever rejects the Son will not see life, for God's wrath remains on them." Jesus Himself said that the wrath of God is on all nonbelievers. You might be wondering, *Wait. How can God be good and loving and still pour out His wrath on His creation?* The truth is actually quite simple.

The wrath of God is not proof of God's cruelty. God is *not* cruel. The wrath of God is proof of God's holiness. His perfection requires everything that is not holy to be consumed. This is not because He is unkind; it is simply because He is perfect. Mankind was never supposed to exist outside God's protection from His wrath. We were created to live with Him in a perfect world, free from His wrath that falls on unholiness. And when sin entered the story, Jesus made a way for us to find our way back to Him.

He took His own wrath upon Himself so that we didn't have to pay the eternal price for our unholiness. God suffered His own wrath, taking on our sin, just to restore His relationship with us. First Thessalonians 5:9 reminds us, "God has not destined us for wrath, but to obtain salvation through our Lord Jesus Christ" (ESV). If you couldn't think of anything to thank God for today, there you go.

The wrath of God is not proof of God's cruelty. God is *not* cruel. The wrath of God is proof of God's holiness.

The one, true, holy God loves you. When Scripture says that His Holy Spirit comes near to us, it is this awesome, powerful, perfect God who comes close. It's this holy God who fills us and is a consuming fire that burns up everything in our lives that is unlike Him.

Do you see now why it is so important to remember this? My friend, without an understanding of God's holiness and the wrath from which we have been spared, how can we fully appreciate the sacrifice of Jesus? And without seeing God as a consuming fire, how are we supposed to feel awe or reverence of His Holy Spirit, who chooses to dwell within us?

The Holy Spirit is more than a bonus that we as Christians get added to our lives to strengthen us or to give us wisdom to know what to do. He's more than goosebumps during our favorite worship song or a little nudge in our hearts. The Holy Spirit doesn't come as some weaker version of God so He can be near us as sinful people.

He is the Spirit of the all-consuming Holy God whom Jesus promised to send. He is the Spirit who dwelled within our

Messiah, who resurrected Jesus to new life and resurrects us to new life as well. And He doesn't just come near us with holy fire. In the next chapter we will discuss how He baptizes us with fire, filling us completely with holy power and purpose. This is the Holy Spirit. This is the God So Close.

Let's Pray

Father God,

If we haven't said it enough, thank You. Thank You for sparing us from Your wrath. We know that we were deserving of suffering, but You saved us. You came for us even though we should have fallen under the penalty of being outside of Your presence. We see how good You are. We see how loving You are. We pause in reverence to reflect on Your holiness. You are awesome and perfect, and in this moment, we are aware of just how unlike You we are.

In Your Word, You encourage us to be holy as You are holy. But we know this is impossible without Jesus' sacrifice and Your Spirit working within us. Help us understand what it means to live a life set apart for You. Help us grasp the depths of Your sacrifice that You, a blameless God, would suffer on our behalf because You love us that much. We are grateful for Your Holy Spirit, who is with us even now. Continue to transform us into Your likeness as we spend time in Your presence. In Jesus' name we pray. Amen.

Let's Reflect

1. In what ways do you think God's wrath and holiness are connected?
2. How do you view the love of God and sacrifice of Jesus in light of what we discussed in this chapter?

CHAPTER 5

THE HOLY FIRE OF GOD

God Manifests His Presence

A few years ago, I was standing in a worship service when I perceived in my spirit that God was doing something important in the room. That morning was like most. The worship team was singing onstage, and the people in the room were pouring out their hearts to God in praise. My eyes were closed and my arms were raised when, in an instant, a shift occurred. Because it happened in my spirit, it's hard to describe. But if I were to make a comparison, this shift was similar to the sensation of an airplane taking off and making a sudden turn. There was a spiritual force, almost a holy weight, that didn't seem to be there just moments beforehand.

I had to sit down. I didn't feel light-headed or as though something was wrong with my body. It was holy. It was good. But it was weighty. I continued to sing along with the others in the room and waited to see if the Holy Spirit led me in some specific way. And then my legs began to shake.

It was entirely uncontrollable. I was sitting in the front row and, while experiences like these had happened to me in the past and I wasn't alarmed by it, I didn't want to draw attention to myself. I tried to press down on my legs, but the trembling extended to my arms. Just as a person might have an uncontrollable tremble when they are cold, this was similar—except this didn't have a physiological cause. It was a physical effect in my body that originated in my spirit. I was responding to the presence of God moving through me.

Passionate worship continued all around me as I sat and prayed. *What is it, God? What are You doing?* I opened my eyes and looked around the room. Most others had their eyes closed, arms extended, and were enraptured in praising the Lord.

It was then that I felt my attention drawn to a woman I knew fairly well. We didn't know each other outside of church, but we weren't strangers either. She was staring straight ahead, and while everyone else was lost in song, she seemed to be lost in thought about something occurring far away. I didn't know her well enough to tell for certain, but my spirit perceived that her heart was troubled.

Put your hands on her ears and pray. It wasn't an audible voice that said it. It was like I just knew to do it. One moment I didn't know what to do, and the next, I did. The trembling in my hands stopped. The shaking of my legs stopped. For a brief moment I paused to consider what I had sensed.

Did God really want me to put my hands on this woman's ears and pray right then? How strange that might seem to others . . . and to this woman! I wondered, *Am I imagining things?* But God answered clearly in my spirit: *Go now.*

I began to walk toward her with complete confidence. I knew for certain God was going to do something meaningful. I just wondered how it was going to unfold.

Still lost in thought, this woman didn't see me approach until I was right next to her. I placed my hand on her arm and leaned in to speak to her over the noise of the band. "God asked me to pray for you. I need to do something different. Will you let me put my hands on your ears?"

She agreed, and then the trembling returned as I began to pray. I can't remember my exact words, but as I prayed, the words came quickly and easily. It was as if the Spirit of God was talking to the Father through me. This was a powerful moment.

When I felt the spiritual weight lift off my heart, I concluded the prayer and returned to my seat. God had surely been in the room all along, but He had also revealed His presence in a tangible way. I wondered if I'd ever get to learn why God had invited me into that experience.

I didn't have to wonder long. After the service the woman came over to thank me for praying for her. She shared that her daughter was undergoing chemotherapy for an aggressive form of cancer and had recently begun to lose her hearing. This mom was desperate for her daughter, who had already endured so much, and God chose that morning to let her know that He had heard her prayers for her daughter's ears.

In later chapters we'll discuss how to listen for the prompting of the Holy Spirit and how to discern when God is leading you, as I listened to Him that day. But for now I want to focus on one specific aspect of this event: the manifest presence of God.

The Manifest Presence of God

We've talked about the omnipresence of God and how He is everywhere all the time. Time and space do not contain Him. God says in Jeremiah 23:24, "Do not I fill heaven and earth?" At every point of our lives, whether we are aware of Him or not, the Spirit of God is constantly with us. There are, however, specific moments when God reveals His presence in a tangible way, making His arrival evident both in Scripture and in our lives today. By definition, *manifest* means "readily perceived by the senses and especially by the sense of sight."[1]

But when discussing spiritual manifestation, I think we can add to that definition, "or recognizable by the spirit." God's *manifest presence* is when He makes Himself known to our senses or recognizable to our spirits. When God manifests His presence to us, two things often happen: our spirits become aware that something is happening, and one or more of our five senses perceive the Lord in a physical way.

> When God manifests His presence to us, two things often happen: our spirits become aware that something is happening, and one or more of our five senses perceive the Lord in a physical way.

On that Sunday, to be certain, God was already in the room before we saw or felt any evidence of Him being nearby. Remember, we talked about how God is everywhere. However, He manifested His presence to me in such a way that I responded by asking, *Why are You here, Lord? What are You doing?* The shift in my spirit translated into a physical response in my body. It later became clear that Jesus wanted to bring reassurance and peace to a troubled mother, but in that instant, I simply felt the Holy Spirit moving in a way I hadn't moments before.

Because I realize that, depending on your background, this may sound strange to you, let me ask you a question: Have you ever experienced the manifest presence of the Holy Spirit? Now, before you answer, I will say that if you are a Christian, I believe that you likely have. Yep! If you have asked Jesus to be the Lord of your life and have given your heart to Him, I believe you've experienced His presence through the

Holy Spirit. Either you recognized what you experienced as God's presence, or you experienced something supernatural and didn't recognize it as the Holy Spirit who had come. Either way, I believe you have experienced the manifest presence of God.

Here's an example of what I mean. Perhaps there was a time when you were anxious. It could have been a stressful situation or maybe an anxiety-filled season of life. Maybe one day while you were nervous or afraid, you simply asked God for help, and He responded by manifesting His peace. You felt this peace in your spirit. My guess is that the peace that came from God went beyond just a relaxed heart. Perhaps His presence caused your shoulders, which had been tense, to drop, and your forehead, which had been furrowed in concern, to relax as the weight in your spirit lifted. You felt the presence of God manifest in your heart, mind, and body but might not have realized it was Him.

Or perhaps on another day, you felt a confidence come over you even though you were previously intimidated or embarrassed. You spoke with a boldness that might have been out of character for you. Your voice had power; you felt your heart quicken, determination flowed through you, and you did what you knew was right in the eyes of the Lord. Maybe you thought it was a wave of courage. Maybe you thought it was something that rose up inside you, but you didn't realize it was Someone who was manifesting His Spirit within you.

Sometimes we attribute moments like these to a sudden wave of serenity or bravery. We think we've tapped into some inner strength or hope or determination, when really it is God's manifest presence in our lives. He's made Himself evident in the exact way we've needed Him, helping us because that is what the Holy Spirit does.

When God comes close, our spirits respond, and there are times when our physical senses are aware of His presence as well. Have you ever been listening to a worship song or praying and gotten goosebumps or been moved to tears? What was happening? Your body was physically responding to the presence of God as He manifested His love and faithfulness to you.

When God comes close, our spirits respond.

Why wouldn't our bodies respond to the almighty God in our midst? Wouldn't you imagine that if Jesus walked into the room, your heart might skip a beat or you might be moved to tears? Why then should it be any different for the same Spirit who filled Him to move in our hearts and draw a reaction from us?

The truth is, I believe that God manifests His power in and through us more often than we realize. And while those moments are great, wouldn't it be even more amazing if we tuned our hearts to God's presence and paid attention to the times when He shows up in some clear way?

My friend, the manifest presence of the Holy Spirit is personal, purposeful, and powerful, and for us to understand how and why He reveals His presence to us today, it is important for us to understand how and why He revealed His manifest presence in Scripture. From the moment Adam and Eve left the garden, our God has continued to carry out His plan to bring us back into His presence. In previous chapters, we discussed how the Spirit of God is like breath or like wind, which hovered over creation. Let's now look at how the Holy Spirit has manifested Himself as fire.

The Holy Spirit as Fire

Scripture says that Mount Sinai "was covered with smoke, because the LORD descended on it *in fire*. The smoke billowed up from it like smoke from a furnace, and the whole mountain trembled violently" (Exodus 19:18). As the sound of the trumpet grew louder and louder, Moses spoke, God answered him, and the people of God at the base of the mountain trembled in holy reverence. Just so we are clear, this isn't a metaphorical story. It is a historical truth.

I can only imagine this encounter the Israelites had with God.

Picture it with me. Let's go back and look at what led up to this moment. The Israelites had just left Egypt after four hundred years of bondage. God had sent Moses to lead them out of bondage miraculously so they might worship God freely. After exactly three months of traveling, mostly by foot through the desert, they arrived at Mount Sinai, the mountain of God. The Lord directed that they must clean themselves and gather at the base of the mountain three days later. When they did, the manifest presence of God came.

The Israelites looked up and saw a thick cloud of smoke billowing up from the mountain, and fire descended on it from heaven. Remember, they weren't far away, looking at this scene as if it were a volcano erupting from a safe distance several miles away. They were standing at the foot of the mountain when it began to quake violently in response to the holy presence of God. They heard His voice and were moved in every sense.

They didn't question whether God was real, because they saw His visible power and work. This was just one of the many encounters the Israelites had with the evident presence of God.

Throughout Israel's history, God made His presence known among them, beginning with their leader, Moses.

The Burning Bush

Moses saw the manifest presence of God probably more than anyone else in recorded history. The first of his many encounters with the Lord was at a burning bush. Do you know this story?

One day, while Moses was shepherding flocks of sheep on Mount Horeb, another name for Mount Sinai, he saw a bush that was burning yet not consumed by the fire.

When Moses went to investigate, God spoke to him. Exodus 3:5–6 records His words: "'Do not come any closer,' God said. 'Take off your sandals, for the place where you are standing is holy ground.' Then he said, 'I am the God of your father, the God of Abraham, the God of Isaac and the God of Jacob.' At this, Moses hid his face, because he was afraid to look at God."

There's an important point to mention here. In Exodus 33:20 God said to Moses, "You cannot see my face, for no one may see me and live." Even angels cover their faces as they cry out, "Holy, holy, holy is the LORD Almighty" (Isaiah 6:2–3). The apostle John reminded us that the only person who has seen the Father is Jesus (John 6:46). However, across the ages God has revealed His manifest presence and glory to His people as an act of love for them. And that's exactly what we see here with Moses.

It was within this burning-bush encounter that God directed Moses to return to Egypt because together they were going to lead the Israelites out from the oppression of the Egyptians.

The Pillar of Fire

When the moment came for the Israelites to be led out of Egypt, it wasn't just Moses who led them out. Exodus 13:21–22 records, "By day the LORD went ahead of them in a pillar of cloud to guide them on their way and by night in a pillar of fire to give them light, so that they could travel by day or night. Neither the pillar of cloud by day nor the pillar of fire by night left its place in front of the people."

Personally, I have heard this story of the pillar of fire so often and seen it depicted in children's cartoons so many times that I too easily forget the awesomeness of this event. I mean, an actual pillar of fire was in front of them. I imagine the newly freed Israelites saying, "Which way do we go, Moses? Just guessing here, but we're feeling pretty confident we should follow that miraculous fire tower."

This pillar of fire didn't just lead them. From this manifestation of His presence, God also protected them. When the Egyptians regretted allowing the Israelites to leave, they chased after them, but the Lord stood in between His people and their enemy as a pillar of fire. He manifested His presence among them and pushed back their pursuers. What a sight that must have been!

Before long the Israelites became familiar with the presence of God with them. God even spoke to Moses in Exodus 29:45–46, saying, "I will dwell among the Israelites and be their God. They will know that I am the LORD their God, who brought them out of Egypt *so that I might dwell among them.*" Did you catch that last part? It's also worth underlining. God brought His people out of Egypt *so that He might dwell with them.* This was the purpose of their deliverance. He wanted to bring His people out of bondage and into a land where He could be with them.

The Fire on the Mountain

In the previous chapter we saw that the holiness of God prevents humans from coming close to Him. So how could God come near sinful people like the Israelites before Jesus' arrival? God's holiness required that the Israelites be set apart for Him. Because God loved them, He gave them the Law to guide their lives and instructions on how to build the tabernacle, which would house His presence.

They followed the Law and built God a place to tabernacle among them, and then something truly spectacular started happening:

> The cloud covered the tent of meeting, and the glory of the LORD filled the tabernacle. Moses could not enter the tent of meeting because the cloud had settled on it, and the glory of the LORD filled the tabernacle.
>
> In all the travels of the Israelites, whenever the cloud lifted from above the tabernacle, they would set out; but if the cloud did not lift, they did not set out—until the day it lifted. So the cloud of the LORD was over the tabernacle by day, and fire was in the cloud by night, *in the sight of all the Israelites during all their travels.* (Exodus 40:34–38)

Read again the beauty of that last sentence. The Lord was with them—"In the sight of all the Israelites during all their travels."

From the burning bush, God revealed to Moses His name and His plan for the nation of Israel. From the pillar of fire, God provided His protection. From the fire on the mountain, He gave the Law so His people could be set apart and He could come close to them. From the altar in the tabernacle—where sacrifices were consumed by the fire of God, which came out from His presence—He offered forgiveness for sins. In the tabernacle, He made His presence known so He might dwell among His people. His manifest presence is seen clearly and for clear purposes throughout these many scriptures.

As I mentioned earlier, His manifest presence is personal, purposeful, and powerful. Everything He does flows from His love and His desire to have a relationship with us. God manifests Himself in our midst because He wants to do something. Sometimes He reveals His presence to guide, correct, encourage, heal, or reconcile our relationships. Sometimes He reveals His presence simply because He loves us. Yet all these purposes flow from His desire to be Father, Friend, and Comforter to us. And when He comes in power today, there is no need to wonder whether He's in the room. As apologist, professor, and author Dr. Michael Brown once said, "There is no more need to announce the presence of God's glory than there is need to announce the presence of fire."[2]

Friend, the fire of God has not burned out. He has not changed and cannot change. This is still the same God we serve! He desires to come close to us, and the Holy Spirit makes Jesus known to us. Anytime you experience a moment with the Lord, you are sensing the nearness of

He desires to come close to us, and the Holy Spirit makes Jesus known to us.

the Spirit of God—the same God who was on the mountain, the same God who moves as holy fire. He is right there, moving in your midst.

Let's pause for a moment and invite Him to come close to us now. Let's ask Him to use us to accomplish His purposes. And let's just enjoy being near the God who loves us enough to free us from our personal bondage so that He might dwell with us and now be in us, just as He has been with His chosen people in ages past.

Let's Pray

Father God,

We are grateful for Your all-consuming fire that burns up all that is unholy. We ask You to burn away all that would keep us living in bondage. Through His sacrifice, Jesus set us free from sin. Help us live in the fullness of what Jesus paid for on the cross. Help us enjoy the promise of Your presence, remembering that Your Word says our bodies are temples of the Holy Spirit. Just as You filled the tabernacle with Your glory, You fill us with Your glorious presence. Lord, we are continually amazed that You, a Holy God, would come and make Your home within us. Help us live in such a way that brings You honor. Help us to be holy as You are holy. In Jesus' name we pray. Amen.

Let's Reflect

1. Have you ever experienced a time when God moved near you or through you? What happened?

2. How do you view the fire of God after reading this chapter?

CHAPTER 6

THE OUTPOURING OF THE HOLY SPIRIT

What Pentecost Means for You

Do you like fun surprises? I love being surprised when I truly have no idea that someone is planning to surprise me. For example, my husband made me breakfast in bed the other morning just because he wanted to. I loved it! It was so precious and has become one of my favorite moments he has gifted me because it was a complete surprise. If he had told me the night before, "Hey, tomorrow morning I'm going to surprise you," I'm sure I wouldn't have enjoyed it nearly as much. Why?

Because when someone tells me they are planning a surprise, it gives my mind plenty of time to try and figure out what they might be scheming. It becomes a puzzle I feel compelled to solve. And when I try and solve this puzzle, one of two things typically happens: either I figure out what they were planning and I end up disappointed that I ruined my own surprise; or, I dream up something far more exciting than what the surprise actually is, and I end up disappointed that what I'd guessed was far more elaborate than what was given. (Y'all, I'm cringing just thinking about how fun I sound to be married to.)

The truth is, surprises are fun, but because of the way my mind works I often find them a bit overwhelming. When I think about how Jesus told the disciples to go to Jerusalem and wait for the gift of the Holy Spirit, I can only imagine what the disciples must have been thinking. Yes, Jesus had prepared them, telling them all about the Spirit of truth before He even went to the cross. But what must have gone through their minds as they waited for this promised Person and coming Comforter? How did they respond to the news that there was a surprise coming?

It was one of the final directions Jesus gave them before ascending into heaven: "You shall be baptized with the Holy Spirit not many days from now. . . . You shall receive power when the Holy Spirit has come upon you; and you shall be witnesses to Me in Jerusalem, and in all Judea and Samaria, and to the end of the earth" (Acts 1:5, 8 NKJV).

After Jesus died and came back to life three days later, He appeared to His disciples and taught about the kingdom of God and healed many people. The forty days that followed the resurrection of Jesus were powerful. John 21:25 says, "Jesus did many other things as well. If every one of them were written down, I suppose that even the whole world would not have room for the books that would be written." But as He prepared to return to His Father in heaven, Jesus told His friends to go wait in Jerusalem for the Holy Spirit, saying, "I am going to send you what my Father has promised; but stay in the city until you have been clothed with power from on high" (Luke 24:49).

This was the promise of the Holy Spirit Jesus had spoken of when they were last together in an upper room sharing a final meal. Remember that scripture we broke down word for word a few chapters back? Just before He went to the cross, Jesus said, "I will pray the Father, and He will give you another Helper, that He may abide with you forever—the Spirit of truth, whom the world cannot receive, because it neither sees Him nor knows Him; but you know Him, for He dwells with you and will be in you" (John 14:16–17 NKJV). It seems only fitting that the disciples were gathered in another upper room, waiting for this gift Jesus had spoken of just weeks before.

The truth is, even though Jesus had told them who was coming, what they were about to experience was beyond anything they could have guessed or imagined.

Outside, the city was bustling. The disciples, along with friends, weren't the only ones who had journeyed to Jerusalem for a particular purpose. All able-bodied Jewish males were visiting Jerusalem to participate in a festival called Shavuot, one of three festivals that required a pilgrimage from all capable Jewish men. Shavuot is also known as the Feast of Weeks, or Pentecost.

During Shavuot, Jews celebrated the firstfruits of the wheat harvest, but they also did something else significant: they celebrated the gift of God's Law. According to Jewish tradition, God gave Moses the Law on Mount Sinai during Shavuot. Remember, the Law was a gift to the Israelites from God because it made a way for them to become holy and for God to *come close* to them before Jesus' arrival. The Law made it so that God could *dwell with* His people.

On the day of Pentecost, He would give another gift that made a way for Him to dwell with His people—and dwell not just with them but also in them.

So picture it now: As their fellow Israelites celebrated Shavuot and the gift of the Law in Jerusalem's streets, Jesus' disciples and more than one hundred of their friends were waiting in an upper room for the Father's gift of the Spirit. Then, "suddenly a sound like the blowing of a violent wind came from heaven and filled the whole house where they were sitting. They saw what seemed to be tongues of fire that separated and came to rest on each of them. All of them were filled with the Holy Spirit and began to speak in other tongues as the Spirit enabled them" (Acts 2:2–4).

Imagine you were one of those disciples, sitting in that upper room with your closest friends, when you suddenly heard a sound like a roaring wind. This wasn't the sound of a strong breeze or rustling in the trees. The noise was violent, and it didn't just go by you. The roar seemed to be everywhere at once, filling the entire house. As you looked around the room, filled with awe and wonder, you watched as what appeared to be "tongues of fire" rested on you and on all your friends. What you heard and saw around you was more than words could adequately describe, and what you felt within your spirit was brand-new.

You felt the same hope and anticipation you experienced when Jesus had been in the room with you just weeks earlier, but it was coming from within you now. As you opened your mouth to praise God in response, a language your mind didn't know spilled out, and you were overwhelmed with the joy of the Holy Spirit testifying of Jesus through you. You weren't just *in* the presence of God; you were *carrying* the presence of God. It was in this moment that you suddenly realized everything you thought you knew about God was somehow even more real as you felt His Spirit alive within you.

You weren't just *in* the presence of God; you were *carrying* the presence of God.

This was the outpouring of the Holy Spirit. This fire in the room on the day of Pentecost was the same fire in the burning bush and on the mountain. It was the same fire that appeared as a pillar of fire and later filled the tabernacle. It's the same fire that came down from heaven on the sacrifices before Jesus was the ultimate sacrifice for sin. And it is the same fire that dwells within you as a Believer today.

Pardon me while I get some Pentecostal preach on, but if that doesn't make you want to give Him praise, we've got some work to do!

The Outpouring Is for All People

The remarkable story of the Holy Spirit's arrival in the upper room would have been incredible enough, but this outpouring of God's power and presence wasn't just for those gathered in that house. Scripture says there were God-fearing Jews from every nation and language who were celebrating Shavuot in Jerusalem that day, and when they heard those filled with the Holy Spirit speaking in their native languages, they gathered to see what was going on. Weren't the men inside Galileans? How could they be speaking other languages? Were they drunk? They marveled at what this miracle could mean, but not for long—because a disciple named Peter did exactly what Jesus had said he would do.

Before going to the cross Jesus had told the disciples, "When the Helper comes, whom I shall send to you from the Father, the Spirit of truth who proceeds from the Father, He will testify of Me. And you also will bear witness, because you have been with Me from the beginning" (John 15:26–27 NKJV).

Remembering the words of his friend Jesus, the apostle Peter stood, filled with the power of the Holy Spirit, and testified, sharing the good news of Jesus Christ: "Fellow Jews and all of you who live in Jerusalem, let me explain this to you; listen carefully to what I say. These people are not drunk, as you suppose. It's only nine in the morning! No, this is what was spoken by the prophet Joel: 'In the last days, God says, I will pour out my Spirit on all people'" (Acts 2:14–17).

Peter continued his powerful sermon, talking about Jesus and His death and resurrection, and the Jews who listened were deeply moved. They cried out, "Brothers, what shall we do?" (v. 37). Peter replied, "Repent and be baptized, every one of you, in the name of Jesus Christ for the forgiveness of your sins. And you will receive the gift of the Holy Spirit" (v. 38).

Don't miss what Peter said next: "The promise is for you and your children and for all who are far off—for all whom the Lord our God will call" (v. 39). Grab your highlighter, because Peter was talking about us. Read that line again:

"The promise is for you and your children and for all who are far off—*for all whom the Lord our God will call.*"

We are those whom the Lord our God has called. We who are Christians have repented of our sinfulness. We have confessed that we believe Jesus is the Son of God and the Savior of the world sent by the Father to restore what was lost in the garden. We believe Jesus died and was resurrected, and we are resurrected with Him to new life as well. And that means the gift of the Holy Spirit is promised to us too.

We'll get into what that means for us in just a moment, but I have to pause and point out something really fascinating. First, look at what Acts 2:41 records: "Those who accepted his message were baptized, and about three thousand were added to their number that day." Three thousand men believed in Jesus because of Peter's Spirit-filled message! That would be remarkable enough, but there is an Old Testament parallel here I want you to see.

Remember, Shavuot was a feast when the Jews celebrated that God gave the Law on Mount Sinai so He could dwell among His people. Well, on the day He gave the Law, three thousand men were killed because they were consumed with evil intentions and did not trust in the Lord. (You can read about that in Exodus 32.) But on the day of Pentecost, when the Holy Spirit came so that God could abide within His people forever, three thousand men were saved! Isn't that a stunning parallel? It's not the only one.

Back in the Old Testament, when the Israelites gathered at the base of the mountain as God gave the Law, the fire descended onto the mountain and everyone heard God speak. On this day of Pentecost, the fire descended onto the people and everyone heard the message of Jesus in their own languages. When the Law was given, God's Spirit could dwell among the people. When the Holy Spirit was given, God's Spirit could dwell within the people. Both events on this day brought God's people closer to His heart, because what He wants most is to be close to us so we can know Him!

> When the Law was given, God's Spirit could dwell among the people. When the Holy Spirit was given, God's Spirit could dwell within the people.

What Does Pentecost Mean for Us?

So, my friend, what does all of this mean for us? Well, according to the words of Peter, the Holy Spirit has been poured out for all people. In order for Him to come and dwell within us, we need to do what Peter told those Jews: "Repent and be baptized . . . in the name of Jesus Christ for the forgiveness of your sins. And you will receive the gift of the Holy Spirit" (Acts 2:38). *Yes, Becky, I've done that,* you might be thinking. Well, then be assured that the Holy Spirit sealed your salvation from what once separated you from God (Ephesians 4:30). He "brought about your adoption to sonship. And by him we cry, 'Abba, Father.' The Spirit himself testifies with our spirit that we are God's children" (Romans 8:15–16).

But perhaps you haven't ever felt filled by the Holy Spirit. Perhaps He has always seemed "out there" rather than "right here." Maybe you've heard about the Holy Spirit's power, but you haven't seen that power for yourself. You've heard others say they are led by Him, but you don't know if you hear His voice for yourself. You believe in Jesus, but you don't sense the presence of the Holy Spirit working from within you.

We know from Scripture that when you accept Jesus, the Holy Spirit comes to dwell within you. But as one of my favorite authors, A. W. Tozer, taught, "I do not find in the Old Testament or in the New Testament, neither in Christian biography, in church history or in personal Christian testimonies, the experience of any person who was ever filled with Holy Spirit and didn't know it!"[1] When the Holy Spirit fills us to overflowing, there is a supernatural evidence of His manifest presence. Did you know that if you want to experience a greater measure of God's Spirit filling you, all you have to do is ask?

I can almost hear you asking, "Wait! Didn't you just say I received the Holy Spirit when I believed in Jesus? Why are you telling me to ask to be filled again?"

Well, consider these words of Jesus: "If you, then, being evil [that is, sinful by nature], know how to give good gifts to your children, how much more will your heavenly Father give the Holy Spirit to those who ask and continue to ask Him!" (Luke 11:13 AMP).

Look at that language: "ask and continue to ask Him." Imagine a water pitcher that is brimming with water. That's you now! Imagine a second pitcher pouring into the already filled container. The original pitcher was full, but it was also being filled. This terminology is the phrase Paul used when speaking to the church in Ephesus about being filled with the Holy Spirit. He said, "Don't get drunk with wine, which leads to reckless actions, but be filled by the Spirit" (Ephesians 5:18 HCSB). In the original Greek, the words translated "be filled" mean "to keep being filled" or "be continuously filled."[2]

Filled Afresh with the Holy Spirit

Peter and John, two of Jesus' disciples, modeled that it is possible to be filled afresh with the Holy Spirit. Shortly after the day of Pentecost, Peter and John, through the power of the Holy Spirit, healed a man who was unable to walk. The man was over forty years old, so many people in the community were aware of his disability. The religious leaders of the day believed that Peter and John were blaspheming God by their acts and arrested them. But the Spirit gave Peter and John courage and guided them in what to say, and the leaders were confounded.

When Peter and John were freed, Scripture says they returned to their friends and told them what had happened. Then they prayed together: "Lord, . . . enable your servants to speak your word with great boldness. Stretch out your hand to heal and perform signs and wonders through the name of your holy servant Jesus" (Acts 4:29–30). And as they prayed, look at what the Holy Spirit did: "The place where they were meeting was shaken. And they were all filled with the Holy Spirit and spoke the word of God boldly" (v. 31).

Yes, Peter and John were filled with the Spirit on the day of Pentecost. Yes, they were filled again on this day. No, that does not mean that they'd somehow run out of the Holy Spirit and needed to be refilled. It means the same thing it means for you and me: we can ask and continue to ask for a fresh outpouring of God's Spirit into our hearts as well. Just like a pitcher already full of water can be filled even more, the Holy Spirit can fill our hearts again in this moment.

We can ask and continue to ask for a fresh outpouring of God's Spirit into our hearts.

That's exciting, right? Let's do something together. Let's ask the Holy Spirit to fill us with His power and love. Let's ask Him to flood us with His holy fire and consume anything in our hearts that doesn't bring Jesus glory. I know we have been talking about this throughout previous chapters, but it all comes down to this moment, when the Spirit of truth makes clear who He is in His fullness, and we either grasp the awesome power of God or we miss it.

Can you feel the Spirit of Christ stirring in your heart? Can you sense Him bringing a new level of understanding to your mind? He's not just out there; He's *right here*.

He is the all-consuming, fire-sending, earth-quaking, life-changing, dead-awakening Spirit of the Holy God, and He wants to fill you with His power so that you can know Him for yourself and carry the truth of Jesus into the world around you.

It's all about His love, remember? He loves you and wants to fill you with His Spirit. This isn't something we have to work for or earn. It's not something we try to make happen. It's something we simply ask for and believe that God wants to give. He wants to be the closest He could ever be with us—by actually dwelling within us!

He is the all-consuming, fire-sending, earth-quaking, life-changing, dead-awakening Spirit of the Holy God, and He wants to fill you with His power so that you can know Him for yourself and carry the truth of Jesus into the world around you.

Let's ask the Father to fill us with the Holy Spirit until we overflow and realize that we aren't just dead to our old sins but are now alive with Christ and filled with the same power that raised Him from the grave. Pray with me or talk to the Father using your own sincere words.

Let's Pray

Father God,

Fill me with Your Holy Spirit, whom You promised to send. I believe the gift of His presence was for me! I don't want anything less than all You have. So I yield to You and set down what I've thought was impossible and any way I've previously limited You in my mind. I won't presume what You can or cannot do in me. You said to ask, so I ask.

Like rushing wind, come and blow through my heart and overflow in my spirit. You are welcome to do whatever You want. Use me boldly. Fill me fully. Reveal Your love in a new way! I want my family to know I am full of Your Spirit. I want my friends and community to be changed as I carry Your love into the world. Fill me with Your holy presence until I overflow with hope. In Jesus' name I pray. Amen.

Let's Reflect

1. After reading this chapter, how would you explain what it means to be "filled with the Spirit"?

2. Have you ever had an experience of being filled with the Spirit? If so, what happened? If not, ask God to fill you afresh with His Spirit.

CHAPTER 7

THE GOD WHO SPEAKS

God Has Not Lost His Voice

It was 2013. My husband, Jared, was working as a welder for our family's natural gas pipeline construction company, and I was a stay-at-home mom of two small children. Jared needed to pick up a part for his work in a town two hours away, and he asked if the kids and I wanted to ride with him. I knew this drive would mean spending a total of four hours with two young kids in car seats, but that day I easily said yes to Jared's invitation. It seemed like the right choice.

The kids both napped on the way there, and after our short errand, we went to the park to play. Overall, the entire day was fairly uneventful—that is, until we decided to stop and get ice cream before heading home.

At the ice cream shop, Jared and I lifted up the kids so they could peek into the colorful buckets of ice cream below. My daughter gravitated toward the sherbets and her brother loved anything chocolate. As my kids took their time examining their options, my eyes were drawn to the young woman who held the scoop and cone, waiting for our order.

Her arms bore the scars of days of pain. I didn't know her story, but I've seen these same marks on the arms of friends suffering deeply. For some, the marks meant sadness. For others, loneliness, self-loathing, depression, or the loss of hope had been the catalyst for those scars. This young girl didn't have a sign that shared her story, but her arms testified that she was hurting and had made the choice to harm herself again and again.

My kids made their selections, and she handed them their cones. For the next twenty minutes, we sat in the booth enjoying a cool treat on a hot afternoon. But my heart was still at the counter. I couldn't stop thinking about this young woman. It was as if I could feel her pain, but I could also feel something else. It was as if I could feel the love of Jesus for this young woman as well. In my own heart I heard every truth she needed to hear to combat every lie she had likely believed:

She is lovable.

She is deserving of kindness and compassion.

She isn't alone.

She feels lost, but she has been found by Me.

There wasn't a moment in the darkness when I was far from her.

I have good things planned for her life.

I heard the Spirit of truth revealing the love of our heavenly Father, and the louder His words rang in my ears, the clearer it became that God was asking me to share His love with her.

The kids finished their ice cream, and we made a quick trip to the bathroom before our drive home. I knew what I was hearing in my heart, but I didn't know what to do next. So I kept doing what made sense. I walked with my family to the truck. I buckled the kids in. I opened the passenger door, climbed inside, and fastened my own seat belt. As Jared put the truck into reverse and began to pull out, I felt this wave of urgency crash over me. "Stop!" I shouted. "I have to go back."

We sat there as I wrestled with what to do next. How was I supposed to approach this girl? How could I show her in just a few minutes how much Jesus loved her and how He has scars Himself to prove that love?

I decided that if the Holy Spirit wanted me to share truth

with her, then He'd give me the wisdom to know *how* to share Jesus' love as well. My husband and I prayed together, and then I went back into the store.

Looking back, I can see it was so simple: just look her in the eyes and tell her, "God loves you and has a plan for your life." But that day was one of the first times I had spoken to a stranger because of the Holy Spirit's prompting. I was nervous. And then something happened. The closer I got to her, the more confident I became that I was doing the right thing, the clearer the words I needed to say came into focus, and the more I was overwhelmed by the Father's compassion for her.

When I stepped back inside she was making sundaes, adding strawberry topping to someone's chocolate and vanilla ice cream. I waited patiently for her to finish, and then I walked up to the counter.

"This must seem pretty strange," I said as I began our conversation. "But my husband and I were in here a few minutes ago with our kids. We went to leave, and I just couldn't. We live two hours away, and my husband had an appointment here in town. I wasn't supposed to come, but I felt like I was led to. I think I came all this way because God wants you to know how much He loves you. He sees you right where you are, working here at this shop. He has a plan for your life, a good one, and He wanted to make sure I told you. Here is my email address and name. You can keep it and use it or toss it, but the most important thing I want you to hear is that Jesus loves you very much."

She thanked me, and I walked out. I wish I could tell you that she emailed me and we became good friends. But that's not this story. The reality is, I don't know what has happened in her life since that day, but I know for certain what has taken place in mine. I have become even more awakened to the Spirit of truth, who reveals the heart of the Father in every situation and circumstance, for my life and for the lives of those He puts in my path.

A Life in Tune with God's Voice

A life awakened by the Spirit of God is also a life in tune with His voice. When God comes close, He doesn't just abide silently.

> A life awakened by the Spirit of God is also a life in tune with His voice.

When the day of Pentecost came and people were filled with the Holy Spirit, they began to overflow with words about Jesus. This is one of the great works of the Holy Spirit; He speaks the mysteries of God to the hearts of God's people, testifying of the work of the Son. This is how we know Jesus personally and intimately.

If we could not hear from the Holy Spirit, then we could not know Him for ourselves, love Him fully, or be led by Him daily. Yes, we have the words of Scripture, which are "useful for teaching, rebuking, correcting and training in righteousness, so that the servant of God may be thoroughly equipped for every good work" (2 Timothy 3:16–17). The Bible is indeed the complete Word of God, and with it we have all that we need to live a healthy and pleasing life in service to Him. But I need to say something: God has not lost His voice, nor has He lost His desire to speak to His children. As a matter of fact, the Father sent the Son so our relationship with Him could be restored, and one of the benefits of this restored relationship is our ability to hear from the Holy Spirit as He continually speaks from within us.

Let's not fly past that. Jesus came so that we could have an intimate relationship with God to the point that He would speak to us from within our own spirits. Isn't that beautiful? The voice that called forth the earth, that commanded Adam and Eve in the garden, and that was like the sound of a trumpet in the fire is the same voice who whispers within us today.

> God has not lost His voice, nor has He lost His desire to speak to His children.

My friend, if we are going to learn how to hear the voice of truth for ourselves, we must begin by looking at the evidence of His voice across the ages. Let's rediscover the voice of the Lord in our lives by first looking at Scripture.

The Power of God's Words

When you think of God's voice, you might first think of sound. But when God speaks, it's more than just noise. He releases His power within His words.

John 1:1–3 says, "In the beginning was the Word, and the Word was with God, and the Word was God. He was with God in the beginning. Through him all things were made; without him nothing was made that has been made." Jesus is the Word of God, and in the beginning, there was nothing else. There was only the Father, the Son, and the Holy Spirit. And then God spoke. Light erupted, mountains rose, and life flowed in response to His command. With His word and His voice, everything we know of the world came to be.

"Light, be!" God declared. And light was. "Let the land produce vegetation." And seeds burst forth in vibrant blooms. Day after day, God's voice didn't just issue instructions; it formed creation (Genesis 1).

Much later, Jesus declared, "Be still!" And a storm obeyed, and peace was restored to the atmosphere over a lake (Mark 4:39). He didn't just speak words. He spoke order and peace because God's voice is powerful, expressing His very attributes.

It's this same powerful and creative voice that also offered personal and purposeful commands to Adam and Eve in the garden of Eden: "You are free to eat from any tree in the garden; but you must not eat from the tree of the knowledge of good and evil, for when you eat from it you will certainly die" (Genesis 2:16–17). This command and the gift of His voice affirmed His love for His children. He gave Adam and Eve instructions to keep them safe and in relationship with Him. From the beginning God's voice has been a gift to humanity, and nothing has been able to stop Him from speaking to us. Not even our sin.

Immediately after Adam and Eve disobeyed God and ate the fruit of the forbidden tree, Scripture records, "They heard the voice of the LORD God walking in the garden in the cool of the day: and Adam and his wife hid themselves from the presence of the LORD God amongst the trees of the garden" (Genesis 3:8 KJV).

I love how this translation puts it: "They heard the voice of the LORD God walking . . ." Voices obviously don't have feet. But the Holy Spirit, called "the voice" of the Lord, releases sound with His presence. God called out, "Where are you?" (v. 9). Adam and Eve responded to His call. It's through this conversation we see that not even sin could silence the voice of God or our ability to hear Him.

God Speaks to Draw His People Closer

Ultimately, our God is the God who speaks. Nothing can silence the voice of the Lord because His voice is part of who He is. I often wonder why some would believe He has said all there is to say. Throughout history, God has chosen different ways and different times to speak to His people, but His purpose has always been the same. He speaks to draw us closer to Him.

God Spoke Through the Prophets

One of the ways God drew His people closer to His heart before Jesus came was through the voice of the prophets. Perhaps you think of prophets as people who foretell what is to come. While this is often the role of the prophet, prophets in Scripture were men and women who heard directly from God and were given messages to deliver to specific people and to God's people as a whole. While priests represented the people to God, prophets represented God to the people. They acted as an intermediary between God and humankind.

We have already discussed how the Holy Spirit spoke to and through Moses, but there were other men God appointed to speak on His behalf—men like Samuel, Elijah, Elisha, Jeremiah, Isaiah, and Daniel. They helped shape the history of God's people as they followed Him and proclaimed His messages that foretold the coming Messiah.

God Spoke Through Jesus

Once Jesus arrived, everything He said revealed the heart of the Father in heaven. As the writer of Hebrews pointed out, "In the past God spoke to our ancestors through the prophets at many times and in various ways, but in these last days he has spoken to us by his Son, whom he appointed heir of all things, and through whom also he made the universe. The Son is the radiance of God's glory and the exact representation of his being, sustaining all things by his powerful word" (1:1–3).

Jesus taught us how God sounds when He speaks directly to us. He taught us how He responds in certain situations. He revealed not just the purpose of God but also the nature of our Father in heaven. Jesus spoke with authority but also compassion. He spoke with power but also tenderness. He corrected and rebuked but also comforted. And every word He spoke was what God the Father wanted us to hear. We know this because Jesus declared, "I did not speak on my own, but the Father who sent me commanded me to say all that I have spoken" (John 12:49).

God Speaks Through the Holy Spirit

When Jesus completed His work, the Father sent the Spirit to continue speaking to us on His behalf. We know this is true because Jesus also said, "I have much more to say to you, more than you can now bear. But when he, the Spirit of truth, comes, he will guide you into all the truth. He will not speak on his own; he will speak only what he hears, and he will tell you what is yet to come" (John 16:12–13).

My friend, it is the Holy Spirit who continues to speak to us today. Jesus revealed the Word and returned to the Father. The Holy Spirit came on the day of Pentecost, as we saw in the previous chapter, and He continues to speak what He hears the Father say.

God Still Speaks to Us Today

If you're asking yourself, "Why does this matter to me?" I'd answer this way: the history of God's voice throughout the ages is only important if we allow who God has always been to shape how we see Him today. His Word says He does not change. He is the same yesterday, today, and forever (Hebrews 13:8), and if He was the God who spoke then, He remains the God who speaks now.

God did not direct the final sentence of the Bible to be penned by human hands and then sit back in heaven with His arms crossed, pointing to the Book He gave us with His lips pressed shut. He isn't an instructor who says, "I gave you notes, so if you need an answer, look there." No! While the Bible reveals the heart of God and the relationship we can have with Him, it is not a substitute for the relationship Jesus made available to us.

> The history of God's voice throughout the ages is only important if we allow who God has always been to shape how we see Him today.

The Holy Scriptures are a gift, but as I've heard it said, the Trinity is not made up of the Father, Son, and Holy Bible. The Trinity *is* the Father, Son, and Holy Spirit, and it is through a relationship with the Holy Spirit that the words of the Bible come to life inside us and guide us daily.

I once heard a pastor say that if God had something to say to him, He would have penned it in Scripture. I didn't have a chance to respond to that pastor, but if I had, I'd have asked him a number of questions.

How did he come up with his messages to share each Sunday?

How did he know what to say from the pulpit week after week? Were all his ideas his own personal inspiration? Was he relying only on his own wisdom, or was he prayerfully asking God what he should share with his congregation? Was he listening to the voice of the Holy Spirit, who directed him to a certain passage of Scripture and then brought to his memory the words he had read in the past? Did this sweet old man truly believe that when he closed the Bible at the end of his study time, the Holy Spirit did not bring additional understanding to his heart? Was it not the Holy Spirit who nudged him to reach out to that member of the congregation, or handle a conflict in a particular way? Was it not the Spirit speaking to him that brought him any understanding of Scripture at all? How did he not recognize all the ways God had led him by speaking through His Spirit?

Certainly the Holy Spirit still speaks to the hearts of Believers today, or we could know nothing about God. The Bible would just be words on a page if it were not for the Holy Spirit speaking to us and revealing the meaning to our hearts.

The truth is, Jesus said the Holy Spirit would testify of Him, and we cannot forget that testimony requires communication. The Holy Spirit speaks from within us, leading us and giving us wisdom. Whether or not we recognize what we are sensing as His voice, it is the voice of the Holy Spirit continually guiding us in spirit and in truth (John 4:24). The voice that created all things, holds together all things, and through whom all things were made (Colossians 1:16–17) still whispers within us.

I think we can all agree that we've established that God has not lost His voice. Now we can start learning more about how to recognize when He's speaking to us, and that's what we'll do in the chapters ahead.

Let's Pray

Father God,

You have always spoken so we might know You. We are grateful that nothing can silence You. Help us remember that You desire to speak to us daily. Even now, the Holy Spirit is confirming in our hearts what is true.

Give us ears to hear what You are saying to us. We ask that Your voice would become so distinct from all the other noise that we would recognize Your voice just as we recognize the voices of those we love dearly and know well. Tune our hearts not just to the sound but also to the power and presence that come when You speak. In Jesus' name we pray. Amen.

Let's Reflect

1. Why is it important to remember that God has not lost His voice?
2. How would it affect your relationship with God to believe He speaks directly to your heart today?

CHAPTER 8

THE VOICE OF THE LORD

God Wants Us to Hear Him

I opened up my podcast app on my phone and began to play an episode of a children's science show. My daughter and I were going to run a few errands, and I thought it would be a great opportunity for both of us to learn on the go. Normally, my phone connects automatically to my car and plays through the speakers, but on this day, that function wasn't working. I handed the phone back to my daughter. "Here you go. You can just listen to the podcast on the phone speaker."

"Momma! I had this idea that I should bring my earphones before I left the house, but I couldn't figure out why I might need them. I wasn't bringing a device that uses headphones in the car, so I just decided to leave them. I wish I had followed my gut."

I smiled. "Do you know who knew that you'd need those headphones?" I asked my daughter.

"Um . . . Jesus?" she answered.

"You got it. Jesus knows everything, and sometimes that little gut feeling, or what we call intuition, is actually the voice of the Holy Spirit, who knows all things and talks to us about even little stuff like headphones."

I loved this moment for her. Just the night before, her older brother, Kolton, had come into my room and shared about a moment he had with God as he was trying to go to sleep.

"Mom," Kolton had said, "I just felt overwhelmed as I was trying to fall asleep." I completely understood. The last three years of his life had involved the challenges of two cross-country moves, multiple schools, and a global pandemic, and his sensitive heart was needing some extra hope. But God had spoken just the encouragement he needed to hear. Kolton continued, "So I was walking into my room and the light was off, and God said, 'Sometimes life feels like a dark house, but I have given you a light. Just turn it on, Kolton. Turn on the light.'"

I just love how clearly my boy hears God's voice. I opened up my Bible and read him two scriptures: one about Jesus being the Light of the World (John 8:12) and the other about Jesus calling us to be lights in the darkness (Matthew 5:16). My son was encouraged not because everything was suddenly okay (because everything was still far from okay), but because he knew that God had spoken to him, telling him Jesus was the answer to everything he faced.

My daughter also had come into my room and listened to her brother's story. While she was happy for him, she felt as most little sisters might in that situation. "Ugh!" she said. "Why doesn't God talk to *me*?"

I reminded her that God absolutely does speak to her. He speaks to all of us. She just hadn't yet learned to recognize how He speaks and what His voice sounds like when He does. I knew she wanted to believe me, but when it seems as though God speaks to everyone but you, it can be hard to trust that God really does care about you as much as He loves those who obviously hear from Him.

The next day, as my daughter held my phone in her hand, listening to the podcast and thinking about the headphones and the conversation we had the night before, she believed what had previously seemed untrue. "Momma! God *does* talk to me!"

"You better believe He does, sister," I encouraged her. "And for you this time, His voice just sounded like a good idea."

Tuning Our Senses to God's Presence

In the previous chapter we saw that God has continued to speak from creation to present-day conversations. For some He spoke audibly, and for others He led through the prompting of His Spirit. Today, His voice continues to speak to us, using multiple methods that we often perceive through our spiritual senses. We just need to learn to tune those senses to His presence.

I am curious. I wonder if as you have been reading you've thought some of the same questions my daughter asked:

Why does God seem to speak so clearly to everyone but me?

How do I recognize His voice in my daily life?

What does God's voice sound like?

What I said to my daughter is true for you too: If you are a Believer in Jesus, you do hear God. You just might not have recognized what you heard as His voice. Jesus said, "My sheep hear my voice, and I know them, and they follow me" (John 10:27 KJV). Jesus also said, "No one can come to me unless the Father who sent me draws them" (John 6:44).

The Holy Spirit has been speaking to you since before you even believed in Jesus, drawing you into a relationship with God. Every step you've taken toward Him was a result of His leading and direction, pulling your spirit closer to His. So we know that your heart hears Him and follows Him. Perhaps all that is left is helping your mind recognize what is happening within your spirit.

How Can We Perceive the Voice of God?

Yes, it would be wonderful if every time God spoke it was an audible announcement from heaven. However, the most common way people hear God speak is supernaturally, using their spiritual senses. Let's talk about how we can spiritually hear, see, understand, or feel God leading us.

Our Spiritual Eyes

Did you know your heart has eyes? In the book of Ephesians, Paul prayed for the Believers in Ephesus, "I pray that the eyes of your heart may be enlightened in order that you may know the hope to which he has called you" (1:18). Paul was speaking of spiritual wisdom and understanding so that they might perceive what God had done for them through the work of His Son. But notice that Paul addressed a spiritual perception that is available to Believers through the eyes of our hearts.

Scripture is full of moments when God's people had supernatural vision. While we tend to think of visions as trances, they can simply be moments when a person's heart or mind sees something that her eyes do not. Our imaginations do this all the time. We imagine a scenario that perhaps makes us uncomfortable, visualizing how it would turn out, playing through all the options and possible outcomes. You've done this before, right? When you're nervous or even just want to be prepared, you think through how something is going to go, watching it unfold as if it has already happened.

The way our minds do this isn't much different from how we might perceive a vision from the Lord. Truthfully, if we really considered how often our minds create entire scenarios from nothing and then watch it all unfold, we would think visions are far less strange.

How common were visions in Scripture? They were so common that when they stopped for a season, it was noteworthy. First Samuel 3:1 says, "In those days the word of the LORD was rare; there were not many visions." This leads us to believe there was a time when there were frequent visions.

Who had visions in the Bible? Samuel (1 Samuel 3), Isaiah (Isaiah 6), Daniel (Daniel 7), Ezekiel (Ezekiel 10), and Zechariah (Zechariah 5) all did.

But visions did not stop in the Old Testament; they continued throughout the New Testament as well. Peter had a vision (Acts 10), and so did a man named Ananias (Acts 9). Visions continued even after Jesus ascended into heaven. The entire book of Revelation is a vision that the apostle John had of the glorified Christ.

What does the frequency of visions throughout the history of God's people mean for us today? I'd like to suggest that God continues to give supernatural vision to our hearts by the power of His Holy Spirit. If what we imagine is something we see with our minds, then why can't supernatural vision be something we see with our hearts? We cannot forget that the unseen world is just as real as what we can perceive and touch around us.

In 2 Kings 6, there's a story about a prophet named Elisha. At that time there was a foreign king who wanted to destroy Israel, but the prophet Elisha heard from God so clearly that he was able to tell Israel's king what the foreign king was plotting in his own bedroom. When the foreign king learned of Elisha's ability, he sent horses and chariots to surround the city where Elisha was staying. Scripture says:

When the servant of the man of God [Elisha] got up and went out early the next morning, an army with horses and chariots had surrounded the city. "Oh no, my lord! What shall we do?" the servant asked.

"Don't be afraid," the prophet answered. "Those who are with us are more than those who are with them."

And Elisha prayed, "Open his eyes, LORD, so that he may see." Then the LORD opened the servant's eyes, and he looked and saw the hills full of horses and chariots of fire all around Elisha. (vv. 15–17)

Isn't that a remarkable story and a powerful reminder that while we have physical eyes that see what is occurring around us, we also have the ability to see supernatural activity through the perception of our spirits?

Listen, I get it. This sounds weird. You might be wondering, *Why don't we hear of people having visions like that today?* To answer that, I'd suggest maybe visions aren't less common. Instead, maybe we have just stopped looking with our spiritual eyes, attributing to our imagination what actually took place in our spirit.

We were living in California when God started talking to Jared and me about moving to Tennessee. We felt that we were being invited by Him to go to the Nashville area, but we were still waiting because we weren't sure. One afternoon as I was folding laundry, I had what some might call a daydream about carrying a small box into a house with a long entry hallway with dark wood floors. I had never been to a similar place before, so this thought seemed out of the ordinary. I decided to write down what I had seen just in case God spoke to me about it later.

When we walked into our Nashville rental house a year later, I realized it was the exact same long entryway I had seen months beforehand. God knew where we'd be, and He prepared my heart long before it happened so that once we arrived, I would have peace that we'd made the right decision to move. Pretty cool, right?

> When God shows us something with our spiritual eyes, it is always for a purpose.

When God shows us something with our spiritual eyes, it is always for a purpose. There is always a message attached to His revelation. Sometimes the message comes right away, and sometimes we must continue to listen for His voice and interpret what He has shown us in the right time.

Our Spiritual Ears

Just as we have spiritual vision, we also have spiritual hearing. When God speaks to our hearts, our spirits hear Him, but it often takes some training to perceive when He is speaking.

Samuel was a man whose life had been marked in service to God. His mom, Hannah, had taken him to the temple to be raised by Eli the priest when he was a young boy, and later on he became one of the greatest prophets in all of Israel.

First Samuel 3 tells us that when Samuel was a child, he heard God calling out to him at night. "Samuel!" God called. Thinking the voice was Eli, Samuel ran to Eli. "Here I am; you called me," he said (v. 5). Eli had not called him, so he directed the boy to go back to bed. Samuel did as he was told, and the Lord called to him again. Samuel went back to see Eli a second time. Again, Eli directed him back to bed. Three times God called Samuel, and three times Samuel went to see Eli.

On the third time, Eli finally understood what was happening. He told Samuel, "Go and lie down, and if he calls you, say, 'Speak, LORD, for your servant is listening'" (v. 9).

Samuel went back to bed and waited on the Lord. This time when God called to Samuel, Samuel replied with the words Eli had instructed him. God then spoke a message to Samuel that would greatly impact Eli and his family. This was the beginning of Samuel's encounters with God, which marked the rest of his life and service to the Lord as a prophet, speaking on behalf of God to the people of Israel.

While sometimes God's voice sounds like a voice, other times it sounds like a thought, a feeling, or a good idea.

Every Believer, including the great prophets of God, has to learn how to discern when God is speaking. The same is true for us. While sometimes God's voice sounds like a voice, other times it sounds like a thought, a feeling, or a good idea.

Our Spiritual Minds

Have you ever experienced a moment like my daughter's when you had an idea that seemed to come out of nowhere? If you're a parent, maybe it felt like parent intuition to check on the kids in the other room only to discover something dangerous was going on. If you're a professional, maybe you thought, *I should bring an extra shirt to work today*, only to spill coffee on yourself later that morning.

We don't always think of these little nudges as the Holy Spirit, but when we become aware that He communicates with us in this way, even using our own thoughts, we realize just how present the voice of God is in our everyday activities.

You might be wondering, *How is it possible for us to know things before they happen?* Well, God knows everything before it happens, right? As we saw previously, Scripture teaches us, "The Spirit searches all things, even the deep things of God. For who knows a person's thoughts except their own spirit within them? In the same way no one knows the thoughts of God except the Spirit of God" (1 Corinthians 2:10–11). The Holy Spirit knows God's thoughts, and as He fills us and speaks to us, we can know God's thoughts too. Scripture also reveals that Believers can say, "We understand these things, for we have the mind of Christ" (v. 16 NLT).

In my life, I have found that the more often I follow these good ideas, trusting that the Holy Spirit sees what I do not yet know, the more often I notice them. In the next chapter we will discuss how to discern when these thoughts are yours and when they are the prompting of the Holy Spirit.

Other People

One of my favorite ways God chooses to speak to us is through other people. I can't tell you how many times I have had a conversation with a friend who said something I was already feeling in my heart. I've had just as many conversations with friends where I have felt led by the Spirit to say something specific, only to have the friend tell me, "Wow! God knew I needed to hear that right now!" We'll talk about this more in the chapters ahead, but for now we need to focus on one important aspect of this idea: throughout Scripture, God has used individuals to deliver His messages.

The apostle Peter was directed by the Holy Spirit to go and tell a large family about Jesus. They were God-fearing, but they weren't from the lineage of God's chosen people. Up until this point, no one knew that salvation through Jesus had come for them as well. When Peter followed the Lord's command and shared the good news with them, they all received the Holy Spirit just as Peter had on the day of Pentecost. They were filled with the Spirit and began speaking in other languages, praising God.

When we think of big moments like these, it can be easy to overlook the similarities between these biblical events and our everyday lives. But the same Spirit who filled Peter also fills you and Believers you know. God still uses ordinary people, full of His perfect presence, to share His messages with the world. So that conversation or card or text that came at just the right time? Well, it wasn't a coincidence. These seemingly ordinary moments are clearly much more significant when we are awakened to the truth that it was God reaching out to us, using His faithful people to pass along His message to us.

> **God still uses ordinary people, full of His perfect presence, to share His messages with the world.**

Our Dreams

In the Old Testament, one man to whom God spoke primarily through dreams was named Joseph. Joseph was loved and highly favored by his father, Jacob (later renamed Israel). Genesis 37:3 says, "Israel loved Joseph more than any of his other sons, because he had been born to him in his old age." This might seem like something that would have made life easier for Joseph, but actually it just made everything harder as he had to endure the jealousy of his eleven brothers. It also didn't help that Joseph was a dreamer and often told his brothers about his dreams.

In Genesis 37:6–8, Joseph said to his brothers, "'Listen to this dream I had: We were binding sheaves of grain out in the field when suddenly my sheaf rose and stood upright, while your sheaves gathered around mine and bowed down to it.' His brothers said to him, 'Do you intend to reign over us? Will you actually rule us?' And they hated him all the more because of his dream and what he had said."

Joseph's brothers hated him so much because of this dream that they plotted to kill him. Then they decided to instead sell him to slave traders, who resold him to an Egyptian official, whose wife made false accusations against him and sent Joseph to prison. I'm not sure it was wise for Joseph to tell his brothers this dream! But God used even these moments of misfortune to continue His plan—for Joseph and ultimately for the redemption of His people. Listen to what happened next.

While in prison, Joseph continued to interpret dreams. Word of Joseph's gifting brought him to speak before the king of Egypt, Pharaoh, who gave Joseph one of the highest positions of power. Pharaoh said to Joseph in Genesis 41:39–40, "Since God has made all this known to you, there is no one so discerning and wise as you. You shall be in charge of my palace, and all my people are to submit to your orders. Only with respect to the throne will I be greater than you."

Famine came to Egypt, but because of Joseph's ability to interpret dreams, the Egyptians were prepared. Joseph's brothers back home, however, were not. Their resources ran out, so they made the choice to travel to Egypt to request provision. When Joseph's brothers arrived, they stood before Joseph and bowed down to him, not realizing he was the brother they had sold all those years ago. In this moment, they fulfilled the meaning of the dream Joseph had had of their sheaves of grain bowing down to his.

I love this story because of how clearly the Lord spoke to Joseph in his dreams and used dreams as a means to promote Joseph to a position of power and provide food for countless people. When God speaks, even through dreams, it reveals His nature. In this case, His purposeful, personal, and powerful voice revealed His desire to provide.

Throughout Scripture, from the Old Testament to the New, God spoke to His people through dreams. So what does this mean for us? He still speaks through dreams today. Have you ever had a dream where you believed the Lord was attempting to tell you something? Have you ever had a friend or family member share a dream that seemed to come true? While obviously not all dreams are from God, we cannot overlook the possibility that the Holy Spirit wants to communicate with our hearts even when we are asleep. After all, His presence doesn't leave us just because we close our eyes. That's something to think about tonight as you prepare for sleep.

His presence doesn't leave us just because we close our eyes.

Nature

Psalm 19:1–4 says, "The heavens declare the glory of God; the skies proclaim the work of his hands. Day after day they pour forth speech; night after night they reveal knowledge. They have no speech, they use no words; no sound is heard from them. Yet their voice goes out into all the earth, their words to the ends of the world." Scripture makes it clear that the wonders of God's creation speak of His goodness. We read in the Bible many times that God used His creation to communicate with His people.

One of the most well-known stories of nature communicating God's heart was when Noah and his family came out of the ark, and God put a rainbow in the sky as a promise never to allow floodwater to destroy the earth again (Genesis 9:12–16). Today, the rainbow still speaks of God's faithful promise to all creation.

Years later, there was a moment when God sent quail to feed His people as they wandered through the wilderness, and through this He communicated His provision (Exodus 16:11–13). There was another moment when the sun stood still so God's people could defeat their enemies in daylight (Joshua 10:13). Through this act of nature, God communicated His strength and aid. Centuries after that, God used a star in the sky to lead the wise men to Jesus (Matthew 2:9–10), and through this sign of nature He communicated His direction.

I wonder if you can think of a time when God spoke to you through nature. Maybe a storm suddenly cleared just when you needed it to, or a butterfly landed nearby and reminded you of someone you love just as you were missing him or her. Perhaps you saw a bird or felt a breeze or even saw a rainbow yourself.

One of my favorite moments when God confirmed a message to me through nature happened several years ago. One summer night, I had a dream where I got out of a slow-moving vehicle and began running as fast as I could to reach the place I was headed. I woke up the next morning with the feeling that God was about to ask me to do something, and I wouldn't be able to take my own slow time with it. He was asking me to run.

As I thought about the dream from the night before, I kept

hearing in my heart, *Run. Run. You're going to have to run.* Just then, I glanced up and there was a roadrunner standing on my front porch looking in my living room window, staring right at me. I don't think I would have been more surprised if Jesus had sat down at my kitchen island and said, "Run, Becky!" (Okay. I probably would have, but that's not the point.) The point is, God spoke to me through a dream and confirmed it through nature as that roadrunner showed up on my porch.

I will tell you this: later that summer my writing and ministry work exploded, and the only way I could get it all done was to keep running forward. Here's another fun fact: right before God asked us to move to another state, that roadrunner showed up on my porch again.

God sent a rainbow, quail, a stalled sun, a traveling star, and that little roadrunner. What has He used to speak to you?

Our Culture

If none of the other examples of hearing God's voice has been a way you've experienced Him speaking to you, then my guess is that you *will* be able to relate to this next one. Have you ever heard a song on the radio that seemed as though it was played just for you? Or maybe you scrolled past something on social media, read a quote from a book, or even saw a billboard on the side of the road that seemed like it was put there so you could see it?

I attended a private Christian college, and I remember one day that was particularly hard for me. The details of that day don't really matter, but I felt as if God was a million miles away. I decided to take a walk across campus to think and pray, and as I did, I came across this little note on the ground. I decided to pick it up because it had my name on it. The note said, "Smile, Becky, God loves you." The note looked old, as if it had been dropped by someone else and left there. But you couldn't convince me that day that God hadn't placed that tiny affirmation of His love right there in the middle of the path just for me. He knew I'd find it, and I knew He wanted me to know He saw me. God uses aspects of life and culture to speak to our hearts because He is not limited to speaking only through what seems spiritual.

The Bible

The most obvious way God speaks to us today is through His Word, and I don't just mean the words on the page. I mean through the inspiration of the Holy Spirit as we read the Holy Scriptures.

First Corinthians 2:14 says, "The person without the Spirit does not accept the things that come from the Spirit of God but considers them foolishness and cannot understand them because they are discerned only through the Spirit." We received the Spirit of God the moment we became Christians, and now He helps us to understand the words we read in Scripture, revealing the heart and mind of God to us every time we open the Bible. We couldn't understand what God was teaching us without His Spirit explaining it. It's as if He is the speaker and also the interpreter.

I understand that a person might be a little leery of supernatural dreams or visions, but when we stop to consider that it is a supernatural encounter every time the Holy Spirit helps us understand a little more about God through the reading of His Word . . . well, it makes all the other supernatural encounters seem even more possible.

The truth is, when we believe that God still speaks, every-thing about ordinary life changes. Or at least, it should. After all, if God has seen the end of all things from the beginning of time, then He has certainly seen today. And if He is kind and loving, which we believe He is, then He knows what is best every time we need to make a decision. He knows when we should turn right instead of left. He knows when we should speak out about something or wait until a better time.

He has insight on how we could best approach meetings at work or conversations with our families at home. He knows how to help us launch that big new idea (which was likely His inspira-tion in the first place). And He knows how to help us speak into that hard friendship, relationship, or situation.

If we have access to the God who speaks, then why wouldn't we listen for His promptings in everything we do? The most obvi-ous answer is, because we don't recognize when He has spoken.

My prayer is that as you've read this chapter, you've begun to think of all the ways you've heard Him speak throughout your life. Perhaps, like young Samuel, you just haven't recognized that prompting or calling as His voice. Before we move on, let's ask God to point to the places where He has previously spoken in our lives so we can listen for Him again today.

Let's Pray

Father God,

Thank You for being the God who speaks. Bring to our remembrance all the moments we have heard from You in the past. Help us use those times to train our spiritual senses to perceive when You are speaking today.

We know that we were made to hear from You, that You desire to speak to us, and Your Word says we do hear You. We want to be confident that You have spoken. Like Samuel, we say, "Speak, Lord, for Your servant is listening." Strengthen us to be not simply hearers of Your voice but also followers of Your presence. In Jesus' name we pray. Amen.

Let's Reflect

1. What is one moment when you heard God speak clearly in the past?
2. In what way(s) do you hear from God most often?

CHAPTER 9

THE PROMPTING OF THE SPIRIT

How to Be Sure It's His Voice

*G*ive *her the four hundred dollars.*

Jared and I were standing at the rental car counter in Colorado Springs, and the Holy Spirit was clear about what He wanted us to do next. We had flown to Colorado to meet with my publisher about an upcoming project, and while we had the rest of our trip planned, we had yet to secure a vehicle for the few days we'd be in town.

As I heard the Holy Spirit's words, I thought of the envelope of cash in Jared's backpack. He had earned it working overtime— long, hard hours away from home. We had brought it just in case of an emergency, but when the attendant of the rental car company told us her story, I knew instantly why we had felt led to bring the cash with us.

"I haven't been home in nearly ten years, and my niece is getting married," she had shared. "I just can't afford the ticket." The minute the words left her lips, I sensed the Holy Spirit telling me to give her the cash. I was sure of what I needed to do next. My only question was, how was I going to convince Jared that the Holy Spirit wanted us to give her the full price of the ticket? It was money he had worked hard for and was likely looking forward to spending on something he wanted back home.

She continued to type, working to finalize the details of our rental. "Guess what?" she said. "You guys won't believe it, but I have a vehicle here I don't usually have. It's just sitting out there in the lot and doesn't have any other reservations on it. I can give it to you for the same price as the sedan." I looked at Jared, who shot me a quick smile and waited to hear what we'd be driving around town. "It's a brand-new Cadillac Escalade. Would you prefer that instead?"

We quickly said yes. It was a fun surprise and definitely an upgrade from what we'd planned to rent, but all I could think about was the money God had asked me to give her.

She printed the receipt and stepped away to grab the keys. Jared pulled his backpack onto the counter, paid with his debit card, and put away his wallet. If I was going to tell him that I thought we needed to give her the money, this was the moment I needed to do it. "Jared," I whispered, but before I could finish, he was already pulling the white envelope of cash out of his bag. He opened the flap, discreetly showed me the money inside, and gave me a knowing look that ten years of marriage could easily interpret.

Of course the Holy Spirit hadn't just spoken to me. He had spoken to Jared as well.

When the attendant came back to the counter with the keys, Jared held out the cash. "We want to help you get back to your family. Jesus wants you to have this money so you can go home."

She stood there stunned for a moment, saying nothing. And then it hit her all at once. The unexpected offering, the realization that she was going to get to see her family, the reality that God loved her enough to give her this gift . . . it was more than her heart could contain. "Can I give you a hug?" she cried, and we easily agreed.

A few months later, she emailed us a photo. She had used the money and made it home in time for her niece's wedding. The picture showed her standing with her family, and I'm not sure I've ever seen a happier woman.

I'll be honest. It's not every day that God invites us to be a part of meeting someone else's needs in this sort of way. I don't share this story because I want to focus on the monetary gift this woman received. I share this with you as an example of trusting the Lord even when His promptings seem unusual. Because sometimes God invites us into situations that don't make much sense, and we have to be sure that He is the one leading us.

We must pause and ask ourselves, "Is God really asking me to do that? Am I sure I heard Him correctly? Is this the voice of the Lord or not?" I have a feeling you've asked yourself similar questions. So, how *can* we be certain it's the Holy Spirit who is speaking to us?

> Sometimes God invites us into situations that don't make much sense, and we have to be sure that He is the one leading us.

From the previous chapters, we know that God not only desires to speak to us but actively communicates with us using many different methods. To hear His voice clearly, we must learn how to distinguish it from all the other noise we hear within us and around us. We must learn how to discern the voice of truth.

Discerning the Voice of Truth

We have already discussed that Jesus said, "When he, the Spirit of truth, comes, he will guide you into all the truth. He will not speak on his own; he will speak only what he hears, and he will tell you what is yet to come" (John 16:13). While this is a short statement, Jesus' words provide a summary for much of what the Holy Spirit says to us and how we can determine if it's His voice we hear.

Notice that Jesus calls the Holy Spirit "the Spirit of truth." He is not the spirit of partial truth or the spirit of mostly truth. He is the Spirit of truth. Period. This means that what He says to us never contradicts the truth of what we read in Scripture. Remember, even Satan spoke to Jesus using partial truths.

In Matthew 4, Jesus had been fasting in the wilderness for forty days when the Enemy came to him and said, "If You are the Son of God, command that these stones become bread" (v. 3 NKJV). The truth the Enemy spoke was that Jesus was the Son of God. However, the temptation came in the twisting of these words. If You are who You say You are, then do something God would not have You do.

Jesus answered, "It is written, 'Man shall not live by bread alone, but by every word that proceeds from the mouth of God'" (v. 4 NKJV).

The Enemy tried to tempt Jesus again, saying, "If You are the Son of God, throw Yourself down [from a high place]. For it is written: 'He shall give His angels charge over you,' and, 'In their hands they shall bear you up, lest you dash your foot against a stone'" (vv. 5–6 NKJV).

Jesus said to him, "It is written again, 'You shall not tempt the LORD your God'" (v. 7 NKJV).

Y'all, even the Enemy knows Scripture and quoted it to Jesus. But Jesus knew more than simply what the Scriptures said. He knew the heart of His Father and what He had meant. Listen, if the Enemy knows the truth and will attempt to distort it to lead us away from the Lord, then we need to know the Word even better than he does. (But that's another book for another day.)

Does the Bible Confirm What I Am Hearing?

So, my friend, to discern whether we are hearing the voice of truth, we must ask ourselves a few questions. The first one is: *Does the Bible confirm what I am hearing?* The Holy Spirit won't lead you away from what God has already stated in Scripture or tell you to do something that the Bible doesn't confirm. Jesus said He spoke only what He heard His Father say and that the Holy Spirit also would speak only what He heard. Within God, there is no contradiction and no conflicting message. So when discerning what you perceive God to be saying, begin with the Word. What does the Bible say about what you are hearing?

Now, here's the thing: Yes, God's Word is the ultimate authority. However, there are moments when the words we hear the Spirit saying aren't plainly addressed in Scripture. Perhaps God is giving you wisdom about how to handle a particular situation with your spouse or coworker. Perhaps He is guiding you in how you need to proceed with a specific life decision. It's in these moments that you and I need to know not only the Word of God but the character of God as well.

This is how Jesus overcame the deceptive temptation of the Enemy. He knew both the Word and the Father in heaven who had spoken. We, too, must know both. If the voice you hear does not affirm who God says He is or who He says you are in His Word, then what you are hearing isn't His voice.

Does What I'm Hearing Sound Like Jesus?

This brings me to the second question we must ask ourselves when discerning His voice: *Does what I'm hearing sound like Jesus?* We have this incredible gift of having access to the actual recorded words of our living God, words He spoke as He walked the earth. He spoke about faith and healing and confusion and boldness. He spoke about following Him and trusting Him. He might not have spoken about what to do specifically when it comes to parenting an unruly child or defiant teen, how to make sure the bills are paid, or how to ensure your marriage is healthy, but He did speak about the importance of family and provision and humility and wisdom.

We know from Scripture how Jesus responds to many situations we face today. So this is a really simple yet powerful question to ask yourself: "If Jesus were to walk into the room, would He prompt me to take that action? Would He lead me to this decision? Is there peace in the voice I hear?"

I have said it over and over throughout this book: The Holy Spirit is the same Spirit who filled Jesus, was actively involved in His ministry, and brought Him back to life after He had been crucified. So when we hear from the Holy Spirit, He sounds like Jesus. After all, there is only one Spirit of truth.

Here's a great test to help you decide if what you're hearing is from the Lord: *when in doubt, say it out loud.* Seriously. Try saying out loud what you believe God is telling you. Does it bear witness with your spirit? Whether it's a thought, a feeling, a dream, or a vision, simply speaking the message we hear can help us determine if it sounds like something Jesus would say. If Jesus wouldn't say it to your face, then the Holy Spirit wouldn't whisper it to your heart.

Does What I'm Hearing Lead Toward God or Away from Him?

The next test to discern the voice of the Lord is to ask yourself, *Does what I'm hearing lead me or others toward God or away from*

Him? One of the primary works of the Holy Spirit is to "convict the world of sin" (John 16:8 NKJV). While conviction doesn't sound like a good thing, when we become aware of what is separating us from God, we can remove it from our lives. The Holy Spirit carefully points out what we need to do to grow closer to God. The Enemy, however, points out what we've done in order to cause separation between us and God.

If you're hearing words that make you feel discouraged, hopeless, or like a failure or disappointment, then you aren't hearing the Holy Spirit. The Holy Spirit continually points the way for us to have abundant life, found in God's presence. When discerning God's words, remember that the Holy Spirit's voice leads us toward greater intimacy with Him. The Enemy points out our faults and attempts to push us away from God. The Holy Spirit always draws us closer to Him.

> When discerning God's words, remember that the Holy Spirit's voice leads us toward greater intimacy with Him.

Does This Message Testify of the Work of Jesus?

The final test to discern the voice of the Holy Spirit is to ask ourselves, *Does this message testify of the work of Jesus?* Jesus said, "When the Advocate comes, whom I will send to you from the Father—the Spirit of truth who goes out from the Father—he will testify about me" (John 15:26). The testimony of Jesus isn't just that He came and died and rose again. The full testimony is everything Jesus has done for us. He came so that our relationship with Him could be restored and we could love one another as He loves us.

Here's an example of the Holy Spirit testifying of what

Jesus has done for us. Have you ever been in the middle of an argument and felt like you just needed to stop and be quiet? Maybe you knew you were right, but the conversation wasn't going anywhere healthy, and all of a sudden, it was as if you were on the outside looking in. You just knew deeply that you needed to quit speaking and simply listen. Sometimes we think we have great ideas when really we are being led by the voice of the Holy Spirit, who is directing us toward peace and reconciliation, testifying of what Jesus made available for us through His sacrifice.

My friend, God does not hide His wisdom from us. He does not speak in riddles or puzzles. He gave us His Spirit, who clearly reveals the heart and plan of God for our lives. He made us with the ability to hear from Him and respond to Him. We were created with the wiring to hear from our Maker! What's remarkable is that God is not only speaking to us but also actively helping our hearts discern what He is saying.

God is not only speaking to us but also actively helping our hearts discern what He is saying.

It's a supernatural work to hear God, and it's a supernatural work to interpret His voice. We have a good Father who sends us kind and wise words *and* helps us understand and know what to do with what He shares.

There is no supernatural process—including speaking to and hearing from God—that we carry out in our own strength. Rather, it is the work of the Holy Spirit, at work within us, who teaches us to discern the voice of the Lord. And the more we listen to His promptings, the easier it will be to recognize when He speaks.

Making Space to Listen and Learn His Voice

If we are going to discern when God is speaking, we must also make space to listen for and learn His voice. There was a time in my life when I didn't call my parents as often as I call them now. I would call and check in occasionally, but it wasn't until I became a momma that I learned just how much I didn't know about raising children and how much I still needed my own parents for . . . well, just about everything.

While I don't need as much parenting advice twelve years into motherhood, I still call my mom every day because I learned something important during the last decade of our daily discussions: having someone you love share her attention and wisdom with you is an invaluable gift.

James 1:5 says, "If any of you lacks wisdom, you should ask God, who gives generously to all without finding fault, and it will be given to you." This is such hopeful news. God gives wisdom generously to all who ask. I wonder, though, if we focus mostly on the asking rather than on the listening for His answer. When we pray and ask for wisdom, do we make space for God to speak? Do we truly expect an answer? I think if we were honest, we'd say most of our prayer time is spent talking to God. But how much of our communication with Him is simply creating space to listen to what He says in response?

What would it be like if we did something similar with someone we love? Imagine if I called my mom to get her perspective on an issue in my life and I spent the entire call talking, then abruptly hung up. "Mom, here's the situation. Here's how I feel about it. Here's what I'm worried about. What do I do?

Help! Okay, bye." Imagine I then expected her to call me back later, when I was distracted with some other task, and just talk over everything else I had going on. That'd be ridiculous! That's not how a healthy relationship plays out.

What do I do instead? I share my heart, and then I pause. I wait. I listen. I believe my mom will answer me, even if it's not the answer I want.

So why do we believe that God doesn't respond when we speak to Him? Do we think He's busy making a ruling on our situation or trying to figure out what needs to be done next? Is He silently waiting for us to figure it out on our own? No. Nope. Nuh-uh. James is clear: "If any of you lacks wisdom, you should ask God, who gives generously to all without finding fault, and it will be given to you."

Ask God for wisdom. It will be given to you. Those are the steps. Am I saying God always immediately replies in a way we can perceive? No. In my own conversations with my mom, I don't demand, "Tell me what to do *now*!" But I do pause to listen for her response. I create space to listen. My friend, are you making room to listen for the voice of the Holy Spirit? If God did answer you immediately, would your heart be fully focused on His voice, or would you be trying to have two conversations at once, expecting Him to speak over whatever else held the majority of your attention?

Ask God for wisdom. It will be given to you. Those are the steps.

The truth is, we cannot discern whether God is speaking to us if we are not listening for His voice. We think understanding is the first step in discerning the voice of the Lord, when, really, listening is the first step in hearing God.

Remember, there is nothing that can silence Him. And His Spirit has led your spirit into a relationship with Him. I believe you do hear Him, but the real question is: How often do you make time to listen so that you might become more familiar with His daily promptings?

I have found that the more time I spend in prayer listening for God, the more He seems to have to say. My friend, I don't share this to make you feel discouraged in what you've missed. I share this because the Holy Spirit wants to awaken you to everything He has made available to you. Again, I remind you that it is possible for you to have a deeper, richer, clearer relationship with Him. He wants you to know with complete certainty when He is speaking. He wants you to be so familiar with His voice that you can tell it apart from all other thoughts or influences. He is a God who can be known, and He remains so close. Let's pause for a moment and pray together.

Let's Pray

Father God,
   We stop in the middle of everything else going on to just listen for Your voice.

_____

_____

_____

On our journey through this book, we have shared our hearts with You. We have asked for wisdom to learn how to discern when You are speaking to us. Now, without any other agenda than to simply hear from You and become familiar with Your voice, we ask that You'd speak to us. We are listening, God. What do You want to say?

Thank You for nearness. Thank You for the closeness available through the Holy Spirit. Awaken us to Your presence and the power of Your voice. In Jesus' name we pray. Amen.

Let's Reflect

1. Has God ever asked you to do something that seemed out of the ordinary? If so, how did you know it was Him?
2. In what ways do you think recognizing God's voice changes over the course of time you spend speaking with Him?

CHAPTER 10

THE DIRECTION OF THE SPIRIT

The Holy Spirit Leads You Today

*W*hen the offer comes in, take it and go.

I was standing at my kitchen sink in Oklahoma when I heard God speak those words directly to my heart. I can't remember if I was cooking or cleaning or doing a little bit of both, but what I heard that night five years ago still resounds within me today.

I didn't fully understand what God was saying at that moment. I didn't know that He was inviting Jared and me to leave the home where we had raised our babies, our families who lived so close, and the beautiful friends who made up our community and move across the country. I just knew that God had spoken, and He was clear.

I was so confident that He had spoken that I picked up my phone, opened my notes application, and typed the words that I had heard. I wasn't sure what He had meant, but I knew that He had spoken in that moment for a reason.

Leading up to that night, Jared and I had been traveling rather frequently to California for ministry trips throughout the year. It was as if God was drawing our attention to the area. Opportunities to help with various organizations kept popping up, and we'd go, do whatever we had been invited to do, and then return home. But something unusual had begun to happen in our hearts each time we boarded the plane to go back to Oklahoma from California.

We were heartbroken as we left.

It felt as if we were leaving our home rather than going home. The moment we'd arrive back in Oklahoma, we'd begin eagerly looking forward to the next opportunity to visit California. Never in a million years would I have guessed that God was about to invite us to move our family across the country to serve at a church in Los Angeles for the next two years. But God knew. And the night He spoke to me while I stood in my kitchen, His plan began to come into our view.

Jared wasn't in the room that night, but he was having his own conversation with God a few hundred miles away. He was on a six-hour drive from Kansas to Oklahoma, listening to a pastor's podcast to pass the time. It was through that pastor's message that God confirmed in Jared's heart what was coming. I'll be honest, Jared is much better at explaining how his part of the story unfolded, but what I can tell you is that when he got home, he looked me in the eyes and said, "I was listening to this message, and I think we are supposed to move to Los Angeles."

You'd think I might have been shocked at that news, but when Jared told me what he'd heard God speaking to his heart, peace settled over me. I knew he was right. God had already spoken to me before Jared even got home. When the offer came in, whatever that offer would be, we'd go.

I could tell you the full story of our move to California, but it would take the rest of the book. So I'll summarize. Just a few months after God spoke to us about going to California, Jared received an offer to work at a church in the heart of Los Angeles. We moved at the end of that year. It was a wild adventure that required faith every step of the way, but it came down to a very simple process. We sought the guidance of the Holy Spirit. We listened for His voice. He directed. We followed. And the process continued daily for the next two years until He spoke again and led us to Tennessee for a year and a half before eventually leading us back home to Oklahoma.

The God of Big and Small Moments

The truth is, the Holy Spirit is the God of big and small moments. He leads us in radical faith adventures and in the seemingly ordinary decisions we make in any given twenty-four hours. Before we were even born, He knew every step we would take, and then when we came to know Him, He filled us with His Spirit so He could lead us from within, guiding us as any good dad would.

What if you were to wake up tomorrow morning and breathe in and out, welcoming the presence of God in your lungs, and ask God to fill you with His wisdom so you knew which choices to make throughout the day? How would the places you go, the conversations you have, and the thoughts you think change if you could keep in the front of your mind the truth that the Spirit desires to lead you? How would you live differently if you had more awareness that He is present and ready to guide you into a deeper understanding of who God is so that you can serve and trust Him wholeheartedly?

A life awakened by the Holy Spirit is a life that is led by Him. Proverbs 3:5–6 says, "Trust in the Lord with all your heart and lean not on your own understanding; in all your ways submit to him, and he will make your paths straight." This proverb makes a Spirit-led life so simple and clear: acknowledge Him and He will make your paths straight. Allowing the Holy Spirit to become your guide is as simple as acknowledging His existence, focusing on His continual presence, asking for His direction, and then doing what He says.

God knows what's best in every area of your life. Every time you make a decision, you can either move forward with your own understanding or seek His guidance and follow the voice of truth.

A Spirit-Led Life Follows Peace

Within the conversation Jesus had with His disciples about the coming Comforter, who would be sent by the Father, He also said, "Peace I leave with you; my peace I give you. I do not give to you as the world gives. Do not let your hearts be troubled and do not be afraid" (John 14:27).

Jesus knew everything the disciples would face after His death, burial, and resurrection. He knew they would be persecuted and eventually martyred. He knew the Spirit who filled them would lead them through some rough moments. But Jesus gave them a gift: His peace.

We, too, have access to the supernatural peace that comes from the filling of the Holy Spirit. This isn't just peace that comes when everything is okay. It's peace that comes from the presence of God even in the middle of everything being far from okay. It's peace from the one who stands on the stormy sea and pulls us up when we feel as if we're sinking. It's peace even when the Enemy is loud and all we can sense are the wind and waves. The peace Jesus offers is a supernatural knowing within our spirits that we can trust God—even when what we see suggests we cannot.

When we follow the guidance of the Holy Spirit, one of the clearest ways to know if we should move forward is whether there is peace. I'm not talking about emotional peace. There have been plenty of times in my life when my emotions don't match what God is saying. I'm talking about noticing *supernatural* peace and following it—allowing the peace of God to have the final say in what we choose to do. As Colossians 3:15 reminds us, "Let the peace of Christ rule in your hearts." In a Spirit-led life, we trust our spiritual senses even when our thoughts go in circles.

> When we follow the guidance of the Holy Spirit, one of the clearest ways to know if we should move forward is whether there is peace.

A few months ago, I had a conversation with a friend who was planning a cross-country move. She knew that my family and I had recently followed God across the country for the second time, and she texted me, along with a few other trusted friends, asking for prayer. Prompted by the Spirit, I picked up the phone and called her instead of texting her back (something I don't normally do).

"Tell me what's going on," I said. As I listened to her share her heart and her fears and what she believed God was saying, I instantly knew she needed to hear the same advice I'd received years earlier. "If there's peace in going, then go," I told her. "If there's peace in staying, then stay. If there's peace in waiting, then wait."

We follow the advice of Paul to the Colossian church and let the peace of Christ rule in our hearts (Colossians 3:15).

Using this guiding principle is the only way I've ever known with complete certainty that I could make a big decision or life-changing move. I might have felt nervous in my body and anxious in my mind, but as long as there was peace in my spirit, I could take whatever bold step the Holy Spirit was inviting me to take.

Remember how the Israelites followed the manifest presence of God in their travels? When the cloud of God's presence remained on the tabernacle, they stayed. When the cloud moved, they followed. The same Spirit leads us today.

We may feel uncertainty, and we may experience feelings of doubt because we are human. But when we follow the Lord there will be a resounding peace within us as the Spirit declares, "The LORD himself goes before you and will be with you; he will never leave you nor forsake you. Do not be afraid; do not be discouraged" (Deuteronomy 31:8).

A Spirit-Led Life Trusts God's Path and Timing

A Spirit-led life not only follows peace but also trusts that God's path and timing are perfect even when His promptings don't make sense. I often think of the Israelites' journey out of Egypt as they trusted a God who hadn't intervened in their situation for more than four hundred years. Generations and generations of men and women had lived and died waiting for a deliverer to rescue them, but it wasn't until God sent Moses that they finally experienced freedom from slavery in Egypt. Suddenly, they not only had a deliverer, but they had to trust this God who had seemed silent or absent for centuries.

Where were you? I bet they thought. *How can we trust You?* I bet they asked in their hearts. But He was exactly who He has always been—a God who is right on time and who leads His children in the perfect direction and timing.

When the Israelites were leaving Egypt, there was a moment when God directed His people around a potential problem. Exodus 13:17–18 records, "God did not lead them by way of the land of the Philistines, although that was near; for God said, 'Lest perhaps the people change their minds when they see war, and return to Egypt.' So God led the people around by way of the wilderness of the Red Sea" (NKJV).

Do you see what happened here? God knew how the Israelites might respond if they met a certain threat, so He led them a different direction. This path, which He knew was safer, brought them to the Red Sea.

The Israelites, of course, were oblivious to what they'd been spared from, and they were quick to feel terrified when the Egyptian army chased them right to the edge of the sea. The people cried out, "Because there were no graves in Egypt, have you taken us away to die in the wilderness? . . . It would have been better for us to serve the Egyptians than that we should die in the wilderness" (Exodus 14:11–12 NKJV).

Look how Moses answered: "The LORD will fight for you, and you shall hold your peace" (v. 14 NKJV).

I love it! "Trust God," Moses was saying. "He has a plan!" The Red Sea was about to open up and form a highway for the first and only time in history. The Israelites would be witnesses to the miraculous works of a God who leads His people exactly where they need to be exactly when they need to be there. They just couldn't see it. They couldn't understand it. They didn't know what they'd been spared from by taking this route. They trusted their emotions rather than the Spirit of God who led them.

My friend, we must cling tightly to peace. God doesn't hide it from us.

A Spirit-Led Life Knows That No Is an Acceptable Answer

This moment with the Israelites wasn't the only time the Holy Spirit said, "Don't go that way." As we live a Spirit-led life, we must remember that no is a perfectly acceptable answer from God, and we need to trust Him when He says it.

In Acts 16 we read about the apostle Paul, who traveled and spoke about Jesus. Paul and his companions were directed specifically by the Spirit: "When they had gone through Phrygia and the region of Galatia, they were forbidden by the Holy Spirit to preach the word in Asia. After they had come to Mysia, they tried to go into Bithynia, but the Spirit did not permit them. So passing by Mysia, they came down to Troas" (vv. 6–8 NKJV).

Listen, I understand that every word in Scripture is included for a purpose. I know there is deep and significant meaning to this part of Church history found in the book of Acts. But for you and me today? Maybe we just need to let these passages remind us that sometimes the Holy Spirit says, "Don't." Sometimes He says, "Stop." Sometimes He says, "Go the other way." The Holy Spirit doesn't just direct us with yeses. He directs our steps with nos as well. But He always leads us down certain roads because He has a purpose. He always guides us with eternity in mind.

A Spirit-Led Life Leads Others to Jesus

I suppose that is one of the most important lessons we can learn as we explore a life awakened to the continual presence of God. The Holy Spirit cares deeply about how the actions of our lives affect eternity, because He cares deeply about seeing Jesus receive what He gave His life for—a relationship with all those whom He would call.

Every day we have the opportunity to bring souls into the kingdom of heaven, if only we choose to share the Spirit of truth and testimony of Jesus with the world. We cannot forget that a Spirit-led life is extremely important not just for ourselves but for those we encounter as well. In every moment He leads, there are others who need us to be sensitive to His promptings. There are always effects when we follow the straight path He sets before us. It doesn't mean our lives will always be free from trials, but it does mean that the lives of others might be changed. Paul proved this to be true.

After Paul followed the Spirit and did not go to the places that the Spirit forbade, He ended up in a town called Philippi. God had big plans for this prominent city in Macedonia. Paul and his companions spoke to a group of women who met in the city, and a woman named Lydia and her entire household came to believe that Jesus was the Son of God.

As they continued traveling through the city, they encountered a slave girl who was possessed by a demonic spirit. Paul spoke to the spirit and commanded it to leave the girl. When it obeyed and this girl was freed spiritually, her masters who'd profited off her ability to tell the future were enraged. Scripture says, "When her masters saw that their hope of profit was gone, they seized Paul and Silas and dragged them into the marketplace to the authorities" (Acts 16:19 NKJV).

Paul and Silas were imprisoned, bound, and chained in an inner cell. But look at how this story unfolds:

> About midnight Paul and Silas were praying and singing hymns to God, and the other prisoners were listening to them. Suddenly there was such a violent earthquake that the foundations of the prison were shaken. At once all the prison doors flew open, and everyone's chains came loose. . . .
>
> The jailer called for lights, rushed in and fell trembling before Paul and Silas. He then brought them out and asked, "Sirs, what must I do to be saved?"
>
> They replied, "Believe in the Lord Jesus, and you will be saved—you and your household." Then they spoke the word of the Lord to him and to all the others in his house. At that hour of the night the jailer took them and washed their wounds; then immediately he and all his household were baptized. The jailer brought them into his house and set a meal before them; he was filled with joy because he had come to believe in God—he and his whole household. (Acts 16:25–26, 29–34)

My friend, sometimes we forget that a Spirit-led life isn't free of trials. Paul answered God's call and ended up in prison for preaching the gospel. Yet his countenance and praise while he was in that dark place brought supernatural life and freedom to many as he shared the testimony of Jesus. He trusted God even while he was in jail—even when life seemed to be far from perfect. There's a lesson here for us.

A Spirit-Led Life Isn't Free from Trial

I wonder if you've ever followed the Holy Spirit and ended up in a season of discomfort. Perhaps you wondered, *Did God really bring me here? Didn't He know it would be this way?* It can be hard to see what God is doing or what His purposes have been when there is pain or struggle on the road He leads you down.

Truthfully, we often don't understand until we reach the other side of that season or moment. But these hard situations aren't the result of a God who makes mistakes. They may not even be the result of our own missteps. Most painful places on the path in front of us are simply the consequence of the whole world living outside of God's perfect presence. Remember, the proverb says, "Trust in the LORD with all your heart and lean not on your own understanding; in all your ways submit to him, and he will make your paths straight" (3:5–6). God will make the path *straight*. Not easy. Not free from problems. Not painless. *Straight*.

He walked with Jesus all the way to the cross, and He remains with us always—through every victory and every valley. He won't ever lead us to a place where He will not go as well. As we follow Him on this adventure of life, we can know that it is from a place of love that He leads. And we get to treasure the reward of remaining in His presence.

Let's Pray

Father God,
We are so grateful there isn't a decision we have to make on

our own or a step we have to take on our own. You don't leave us to our own judgment and limited knowledge about how to move forward. We just want to stop and say thank You for the gift of Your leadership. Thank You for guiding us from within.

Help us see the value of trusting You to lead us down roads that might not always be the ones we'd choose, believing that You have our best interest at heart. Fill us afresh with Your Spirit so we might follow Him boldly. In Jesus' name we pray. Amen.

Let's Reflect

1. Can you think of a time when you sensed peace in making a decision? What happened?
2. Have you ever experienced a time when God led you in a direction that didn't make sense? If so, what was the outcome of following Him?

CHAPTER 11

THE PROPHETIC WORD

How to Hear God for Others

The evening conference session was about to begin, and once again, I felt the familiar presence of the Holy Spirit exceptionally close. I had flown across the country to attend a women's event held at one of my favorite churches. I had long admired this church's teaching and emphasis on the Word of God and the power of the Holy Spirit to reveal the love of Jesus; however, I had never actually visited in person. I was so glad finally to have the opportunity.

I had made a last-minute decision to go, and I didn't even have a chance to invite a girlfriend to come with me. I was on my own. As a young momma, I really did enjoy the break and the idea of a few days to myself. I hoped the weekend would give me time to be refueled and refreshed before I returned home.

The lights dimmed, and the leader invited us into a moment of prayer before the service started. She said, "Let's just take a second and settle our hearts and affections on Jesus. Let's leave everything that would steal our focus away from Him. We're not here to fixate on our families, our responsibilities, our jobs, or what's waiting for us at the end of this weekend. We are here simply to meet with God and hear from Him."

As my eyes were closed and I thought about Jesus and how much I wanted a fresh filling of God's Spirit that weekend, I suddenly pictured in my mind a tall, bald man with two young children standing next to him. It wasn't a clear picture. I couldn't really make out a face. I simply knew the person I was seeing was bald, and the children barely came up to his waist. I had never seen this person before. I didn't recognize the kids either. But I instantly knew exactly who he was.

I turned to the woman sitting next to me. We didn't know each other, but the Holy Spirit told me that I had just perceived a picture of her husband and children. God had a message He wanted me to share with her. As the conference leader concluded her prayer and the worship team began their first song, I leaned over to my seat neighbor and introduced myself.

"Hi. I'm Becky," I said, and she told me her name as well. "I have a question," I began. "Is your husband bald by any chance?" She chuckled nervously and looked at her friend seated on the other side of her. "Yes?" she answered curiously. I continued, "Do you have two young children as well at home?" She said she did, and tears formed in her eyes. The Holy Spirit was inviting us both into a tender moment.

I said to her, "Jesus wants you to know that they're going to be okay this weekend. He knows you're worried about them, but the Holy Spirit is with them, and you can focus on what's going on here, knowing that He has it all under control back home."

She cried and cried. It's a powerful realization to know that God actually sees us, cares about what weighs on our hearts, and wants to help. I smiled and turned back to the front, trusting that if the Holy Spirit was already speaking to me so clearly, the rest of the weekend would be just as encouraging.

While I've had other amazing encounters with the Spirit of God, this is one of my favorites because it was the first time God had given me a specific message to share with someone else and had shown me details about their life to confirm that what He was telling me was true. Yes, I had heard Him speak clearly to me before that moment, but when He chose to speak through me, I discovered a new way of knowing Him. I didn't just know of His love for *me*. He was teaching me about how to see and share His love for others.

As we've discussed throughout this book, when the Holy Spirit speaks to our hearts, He doesn't just speak to us about our own lives. He can speak to us about anything, and sometimes He asks us to share what we hear with those He brings into our path. When we pass along God's messages for the world around us, we are speaking *prophetically*.

Have you heard that term before? It's understandable that you might have all sorts of thoughts that come to your mind when you read the word *prophetic*. I mean, first I tell you that you can hear God, then I tell you that you can hear God for other people, and now I tell you that when you speak those messages you hear you're acting as a prophet. You might think, *I'm not a prophet. I know about prophets in the Bible, and I'm not like them.* But I believe that prophetic ministry is widely misunderstood, and I want to bring some clarity to one of the ways that the Holy Spirit moves in us and through us.

The Role of Prophetic Messages

Let me start by pointing to a specific passage of Scripture I'd like you to keep in the back of your mind as I explain the role of prophetic messages today.

In Paul's first letter to the Corinthian church, he gave a specific teaching about how to live a life filled with God's Spirit and be used by Him for His work. Paul taught about special giftings that the Holy Spirit gives those He fills. We'll talk more about those spiritual gifts later. For now, focus on this one statement. Paul said, "Follow the way of love and eagerly desire gifts of the Spirit, especially prophecy" (1 Corinthians 14:1). He went on to say, "The one who prophesies speaks to people for their strengthening, encouraging and comfort" (v. 3).

I'm sure you've caught on by now that I like to repeat myself so we don't miss the most important thoughts shared on these pages. So let's look at part of that statement carefully. Read it again slowly.

The one who prophesies speaks to people for their strengthening, encouraging, and comfort.

What does that scripture mean for us today? Let's look back at what the Bible teaches us about prophets and their messages so we can better understand how Paul's statement applies to our lives.

The Role of a Prophet in the Old Testament

In previous chapters, we briefly discussed the role of the prophet in the Old Testament, the time before Jesus was born. Remember, prophets back then were men who represented God to the people—listening to the Lord and then sharing what they heard. Sometimes they spoke to individuals, and sometimes they spoke to the nation of Israel. In the Old Testament, we find these men chosen by God, called to a life of familiarity with His voice, and used in specific ways to share what God wanted to say.

During this time, humanity didn't yet have what you and

I possess. Jesus had not come to reconcile men back to God. There was separation. Men and women couldn't hear God clearly for themselves unless God chose to speak to them, because Jesus hadn't yet come, and the Holy Spirit hadn't yet been poured out for all Believers on the day of Pentecost. However, God desired to guide His people, so He used the prophets to do that.

This was a heavy calling. If God's people wanted to follow the Lord or know His wisdom, they had to rely on what a prophet directed them to do. The weight of the nation of Israel hung in the balance as a prophet aimed to hear and retell God's messages accurately and completely. While the prophet's life was spent in close relationship with God, it was often burdened by the task of speaking sharp and rebuking words. Can you imagine being the prophet who had to tell people that God was displeased and change was required? Can you imagine having to deliver a message of warning?

Speaking on behalf of God has always carried a great responsibility; this certainly has not changed. But throughout history, God has entrusted ordinary people with the task of being His mouthpiece. One of the clearest examples of the function of a prophet is defined by God in a few conversations He had with Moses. Do you remember how we discussed earlier that God manifested His

Throughout history, God has entrusted ordinary people with the task of being His mouthpiece.

presence to Moses through a burning bush and directed him to return to his people? During that conversation, Moses argued a bit, saying to the Lord, "Pardon your servant, Lord. I have never been eloquent, neither in the past nor since you have spoken to your servant. I am slow of speech and tongue. . . . Please send someone else" (Exodus 4:10, 13). Their conversation went back and forth before the Lord finally said to Moses, "What about your brother, Aaron the Levite? I know he can speak well. He is already on his way to meet you, and he will be glad to see you. You shall speak to him and put words in his mouth; I will help both of you speak and will teach you what to do" (vv. 14–15).

Look at the order of communication. God originally intended to speak to His people through Moses. Moses would act as a prophet. However, Moses was uncomfortable and wasn't skilled in speech. So God sent Aaron to help Moses. Now God would speak to His people through Moses, who spoke through Aaron.

God said, "He [Aaron] will speak to the people for you, and it will be as if he were your mouth and as if you were God to him" (v. 16). Just as God gave Moses words to say, Moses would give Aaron words to say.

You'd think this might settle the issue for Moses, but a little later on, God spoke to Moses again and told him to share a message with the king of Egypt. Moses reminded God of his "faltering lips" (Exodus 6:30), and God said, "See, I have made you like God to Pharaoh, and your brother Aaron will be your prophet. You are to say everything I command you, and your brother Aaron is to tell Pharaoh to let the Israelites go out of his country" (Exodus 7:1–2).

In this passage, we see how God calls the intermediary position of relaying messages from one person to another a prophet. In our lives today, God gives us the ability to relay messages from Him to the people He puts in our path as well.

The Role of Prophecy Today

No longer are there only specific men or women who hear from God and are responsible for the entire nation. No longer does God select only specific men to hear His voice intimately. One of the most astounding gifts God gave us is the continual presence of His Spirit within us, the Spirit who testifies of the works of Jesus. Remember, Scripture teaches us that the Holy Spirit speaks only what He hears (John 16:13). He is always prophesying the truth of God to our hearts. He is the one who declares the mysteries of God directly to us.

He is always reminding us of what God has already accomplished through Jesus. He is always speaking of the Father's love for us. He is always guiding us toward Him and away from sin. And when we interact with others around us, we have the ability to hear the truth that God has to say about them and say it out loud.

Simply put, we have the ability to listen to the Holy Spirit and prophesy the good news of Jesus.

Think of yourself as a conduit whose job is simply to relay what you hear God saying. What does God want to tell your family? What does He want to say to your friends? What does God want to say to your neighbors or coworkers?

When we think of prophecy, we often think only of God revealing information about future events. While God still uses us to speak about what He will do in the future, there are plenty of times when what we prophesy reveals the heart of God to others about what they are facing right now, this minute, today. An example of this would be the conversation I had with the young woman at the ice cream counter. I heard what the Spirit of truth was saying, and when I shared it with her, I was prophesying the testimony of Jesus for her.

When we prophesy, we declare the truth we hear God saying. We become His mouthpieces; He uses our lips and our voices to convey His heart. And just as He did with the prophets in the Old Testament, He speaks with the purpose of drawing people closer to Him!

What a special opportunity from the Lord to be the carriers of His love and sharers of His truth with the world. Just as we create space to listen for the prompting of the Holy Spirit in our lives, we can listen for what God is saying about those around us as well.

Hearing God's Voice for the World Around Us

So how do we hear God's voice for the world around us? Here are some practical ways He might speak to us. The Holy Spirit might bring someone to your mind. You might hear God speak to your spiritual ears or show something to your spiritual eyes. You might hear a simple word or see a picture. You might have a feeling about someone you know. You might even have a dream. In nearly every way we might hear God speak to us about ourselves, we can hear God speak to us about others.

A few years ago, I received an email from a pastor friend of mine. He said that he had woken up that morning in the early hours of the day, and the Lord had shown him a picture of me standing in front of a large door. There was light shining all around it, and in the vision the door was about to open. He knew in his spirit that God was saying a large opportunity was coming for me, and this opportunity was part of God's plan for me. Because this friend knows the voice of the Lord clearly, and I trust his relationship with God, I wrote down everything my friend said and began to pray about it.

I prayed, *Lord, help me recognize this opportunity when it comes. Do whatever is necessary for that door to open. I trust You and Your timing. Thank You for knowing what is coming for me even when everything seems uncertain from my perspective. Give me Your eyes to see.*

At the time, our family's finances were uncertain. We had just moved from California to Tennessee, trusting that God had led us to another new city for a purpose, but we couldn't quite see why yet. His plan wasn't obvious, and we were wondering, *Did we miss something? Did God really bring us here for a reason?* When my friend shared the vision with me, it encouraged and comforted me. Just knowing that God had some unseen plan and a future opportunity that would be revealed any moment brought me so much peace. The message strengthened my heart and helped me continue to trust the Lord to do whatever He was doing. I felt the love of God, even before I had any answers or my situation changed.

It didn't take long for God to reveal the meaning of the vision. Less than a month later, my literary agent emailed me with exciting news. A publishing house based out of Nashville wanted to meet with me. They had been following my writing career and were hopeful we'd get to work together. By the end of the week, I received an unexpected offer from the publisher for this very book you hold in your hands. The door in the dream symbolized the opportunity to write this work and share this message. And because God had already shared with me that this opportunity was from Him, when the offer came, I had complete peace in following the Holy Spirit to sign the contract and begin this work.

Do you see how powerful it is to create space to listen for God speaking about those we know and love? Do you see how such a simple act of obedience on our part can bring so much hope as the Holy Spirit speaks to others through us?

I feel like the Holy Spirit is so happy we are talking about this. I feel like He is stepping out from the shadows where we asked Him to stay and is saying, *Do you see Me now? Do you see what we can do together? If Jesus were to tell you to go and share good news, you would! Can't you see who is speaking to you now? Can't you see what you get to be a part of? I have people I want to share My love with. I have specific messages I want you to tell others. You do hear My voice! You do recognize it. Listen, My love. Listen to Me, and I will share My heart with you.*

Does What I'm Hearing Strengthen, Encourage, and Comfort?

So how do we listen and respond to the Holy Spirit? How do we practically know how to speak prophetically on behalf of God? It's a process you know well from previous chapters. You begin by listening. You learn the voice of the Lord, and when you believe you hear God speaking to you for someone else, you ask yourself all the same questions that you considered when discerning the voice of the Lord in your own life:

- *Does the Bible confirm what I am hearing?*
- *Does what I'm hearing sound like Jesus?*
- *Does what I'm hearing lead this person toward God or away from Him?*
- *Does this message testify of the work of Jesus?*

When we share what we hear God saying for others, we must ask ourselves a couple more questions: *Does what I'm hearing strengthen, encourage, and comfort? Does it reveal the love of God who would send His Son to die for this person?*

Prophecy and love go hand in hand because everything the Father speaks to us through His Spirit is motivated by His love for us. I learned from Shawn Bolz, a well-known authority on this subject, that we cannot accurately share God's heart or message with someone if we don't understand and share His love for that person first. Think about it: we can only be a conduit if we pass along what is coming from one source to another. If we haven't received the message of God's love for someone, then how could we possibly pass it on to them? Can you imagine trying to convey a message full of encouragement or hope to someone without feeling the love of God that motivated that message?

Does what I'm hearing strengthen, encourage, and comfort? Does it reveal the love of God who would send His Son to die for this person?

I imagine it would be similar to an annoyed sibling given the task of delivering a message to their brother's or sister's crush: "Hi. They want me to tell you that they really, really like you, and they hope you like them too. If you do, meet them at the front of the building after school. Okay, bye." Sure, the words would be right, but the passion that created them would be lost in translation. And without the passion, the words can become distorted and don't carry their full meaning. Only with love can we speak the full truth.

I'd like you to think for just a moment. Have you ever felt compassion for someone and wanted to share an encouraging word with her? Have you ever felt hope for someone who seemed discouraged and wanted to remind her what the Bible said about the situation she faced? Maybe you had a dream or a picture in your mind, or heard the Holy Spirit say, "Do this. . . . Share this. . . . Offer that."

Only with love can we speak the full truth.

I believe you have likely already had a prophetic moment with the Holy Spirit, speaking on His behalf for someone you know. Perhaps you just thought you were being encouraging. Perhaps you just thought you were bringing comfort. Maybe you didn't even know that your words or actions were a form of prophecy. I have found that when the Spirit of God is inside us, we often experience moments with Him that we don't have language for or an understanding of just yet. After all, He doesn't need us to understand completely who He is or how He works in order to have permission to move in our lives. When He comes, He brings all of Himself to fill us.

However, now that you do understand exactly who desires to speak to the world through you, you have an opportunity to grow in this. You have the chance to eagerly desire the ability to see others as God sees them, to love them as God loves them, and to be the mouthpiece that God uses to speak truth to someone at just the right time.

My friend, it is a weighty responsibility to hear from God for others. But it is a beautiful opportunity given to us by the Holy Spirit that requires us to lean into our relationship with Him, and it reminds us just how close He really is.

Let's Pray

Father God,

Thank You for the continual gift of Your voice in our lives. We recognize that every good thing You've given us, including hearing from You, is a gift that is not just for our benefit but for the good of others too. Teach us how to hear You clearly for the world around us. Teach us how to step out in faith and boldness to share Your messages with those You love. We are ready to be used as conduits, positioned to pass along Your words. With reverence and humility, we simply say that we will aim to listen fully so we can share completely. In Jesus' name we pray. Amen.

Let's Reflect

1. Can you think of a time when you shared something with a friend or loved one that you can see now was likely the prompting of the Holy Spirit? What happened?
2. In your own words, why do you suppose prophecy is something we should eagerly desire?

CHAPTER 12

THE KNOWLEDGE OF GOD

Things Only God Could Know

A few years ago, I woke up one Sunday morning in California and said to my kids, "We cannot be late to church this morning. God has a message for us, and we cannot miss it." Now, I think it would be wonderful if every Sunday morning (or every morning for that matter) we woke up with the same expectation that God had something important He wanted to tell us. But that particular morning, I wasn't just excited about the pastor's message; I *knew* in my spirit that God was going to use the special guest to deliver a message for us. I knew it within me as I knew my own name. I felt like I had an appointment to receive a letter straight from heaven, and I needed to be there to pick it up.

Jared had already driven to the church, since he had to be there early to prepare for the service in Los Angeles. The kids and I drove separately. My entire drive down Interstate 5 into Glendale, I prayed with an overwhelming feeling of hope. *God, whatever happens this morning, I have an expectation that You want to meet with me. There's nothing I want more, Lord. Thank You for whatever it is You're about to do.*

The building was packed, since so many people had come to hear the guest speaker. Rather than sit in a highly sought-after chair, I decided to spend the service with Jared back in the media room, where he coordinated the online streaming services and directed the cameras at the front. Even in the corner room, I sensed something unique was about to happen. The speaker had a great message, and as he began to draw his talk to a close, he said that he wanted to wait and see if God had anything specific He wanted to say or do before he ended.

The man began to pray, and the Holy Spirit began to speak through him. The Spirit showed him two different people in the room and gave him two specific messages to share with them. The man shared faithfully, and those he was speaking to were encouraged, and those in attendance were blessed that God was using this man to share His heart.

As I watched on the monitor, I saw the man pause and look toward the ground. *He's going to give you a message from Me,* the Holy Spirit said in my spirit. I jumped up, turned to Jared, and said, "I have to get out there. He's going to say something specifically about us!"

I walked out of the room and stood at the back of the small auditorium just as the guest speaker said, "As I'm praying, I'm only hearing three letters: *J, K, K.* And it's as if your story began twelve years ago."

The Holy Spirit had already told me that this man had a message for me, but when I heard those three letters and something about twelve years, it confirmed what I already knew was true. My children's names are Jaxton, Kadence, and Kolton, and at that time Jared and I had just celebrated twelve years of marriage.

The man asked if what he was saying made sense to anyone in the room, and everyone waited to see what God was doing. Confident, I announced from the back, "I think you're talking about me!"

The man asked, "Are you musical?"

Suddenly, I wasn't so sure. I'm not musical at all. This certainly wouldn't be something that God would use to confirm that He had a specific message just for us. Perhaps if he had asked, "Are you a writer?" I would have been reassured, but musical?

"No!" I answered from across the room. "I don't think what you have to share is for me after all."

"Well, does the word *cadence* mean anything to you?" He had no idea my daughter's name was Kadence. He thought I must be musical because the Holy Spirit was telling him something about musical cadence, but really the Holy Spirit had told him the name of my kid.

"Kadence is my daughter's name!" I shouted. Everyone cheered. God was speaking, and faith immediately began to rise in the hearts of all who were hearing.

Jared came out from the media room, and we walked to the front together. The guest speaker then told us a very special message from the Lord about our lives and our ministry, what God was calling us to do next, and how the Lord felt about us. He gave us a long message from God, but when he said, "The Lord has seen your sacrifice," I felt like Father God had placed His arms around me and said, "I know, Daughter. I saw what you gave. It was worth it. I know what I'm doing, and I'm proud of you."

This man had no idea we had recently given everything we owned, all that was in our bank accounts, and left behind both of our families to move to California just a year earlier. He had no idea all we had laid down in order to pick up the invitation to follow God, but our heavenly Father had seen it all. The Holy Spirit knew, and He had given this man from Australia a specific word of encouragement and direction for us. It truly marked our lives, drawing us closer to the Lord and reminding us God had a very good plan that we could continue to trust.

The Benefits of Spiritual Knowledge for Others

Have you ever experienced a moment when the Holy Spirit told you something that only He could know? Maybe it wasn't an event quite like this, but perhaps you just knew what a coworker or friend needed to hear and said it at just the right time. Maybe you just knew what your children had really been up to when they said they were doing something else. Maybe you almost felt as though you knew what someone you love was thinking before they even said it. Did you know that the Holy Spirit can reveal information to our hearts that our minds haven't learned?

Remember, Scripture says, "The Spirit searches all things, even the deep things of God. For who knows a person's thoughts except their own spirit within them? In the same way no one knows the thoughts of God except the Spirit of God" (1 Corinthians 2:10–11). We agree and believe that God knows everything. He knows what is happening in the other room, what is happening on the other side of the planet, and what you're going to have for lunch tomorrow. He knows every step you will take until you meet Him in eternity.

There is nothing unknown to the Spirit of God, and He dwells within us. Scripture goes on to say, "What we have received is not the spirit of the world, but the Spirit who is from God, so that we may understand what God has freely given us" (v. 12).

Here's the thing: if God knows all things, and if He speaks to us and through us, then we can be confident that there are moments He may tell us something that only He could know.

Spiritual Knowledge Creates Opportunities for Faith to Rise

Do you remember the story we discussed previously about Elisha asking the Lord to open his servant's spiritual eyes so he could see the supernatural armies surrounding them? They were greater than the enemy armies the Israelites were facing that day, and God enabled both Elisha and his servant to see them (2 Kings 6:17). Elisha also had been able to tell Israel's king what a foreign king was plotting in his own bedroom. Why? Because he'd received special revelation and knew information that only the Spirit of God could know and tell him.

This ability to know facts revealed by the Holy Spirit isn't unique to Elisha's story. Jesus modeled how a person's life can be transformed when the Holy Spirit sees the details no one else does and then speaks about them.

In John 4, Jesus encountered the Samaritan woman. There was a moment during their conversation when Jesus spoke about something only He could know about this woman's private life:

> Jesus modeled how a person's life can be transformed when the Holy Spirit sees the details no one else does and then speaks about them.

He told her, "Go, call your husband and come back."

"I have no husband," she replied.

Jesus said to her, "You are right when you say you have no husband. The fact is, you have had five husbands, and the man you now have is not your husband. What you have just said is quite true."

"Sir," the woman said, "I can see that you are a prophet." (vv. 16–19)

Their conversation continued. When Jesus revealed to her that He was more than a prophet, that He was the actual Messiah sent by His Father, she ran to tell her entire town. Look what she said to the townspeople: "Come, see a man who told me everything I ever did. Could this be the Messiah?" (v. 29).

Jesus didn't just see the woman standing in front of Him; He saw the intimate details of her life. He saw the painful places and the secret places. And when she understood who was speaking to her, it wasn't just her life that was changed—it was her entire town.

We may have been taught that Jesus knows the numbers of hairs on our heads (Matthew 10:30), but there is a big difference between Jesus knowing the hairs on everyone's heads and Jesus specifically knowing the hairs on your head. This realization that Jesus intimately knows us is life changing. It shows us that we matter, and that God hasn't been distant or distracted or uninterested in the details of our lives. He saw it all. He sees it all. And it brings our perspective of Him even closer.

Spiritual Knowledge Creates Opportunities for Spiritual Healing or Encouragement

In the previous chapter, I shared the story of a woman who had a bald husband and two young children. I didn't know her, but the Spirit did. I didn't know her husband or her children, but the Spirit did. And because I knew the Spirit and understood how He spoke to me, I was able to hear from Him and pass along an important message that the Holy Spirit revealed.

The apostle Peter, one of Jesus' followers and best friends, had a similar moment of spiritual knowledge. He had been following Jesus for some time, and he believed that Jesus was the promised Messiah. But Peter had not expressed what he had been taught by the Holy Spirit until Jesus turned to him and said, "Who do you say I am?" Scripture records that Peter answered, "You are the Messiah, the Son of the living God" (Matthew 16:15–16). Jesus replied, "Blessed are you, Simon son of Jonah, for *this was not revealed to you by flesh and blood, but by my Father in heaven*" (v. 17).

This encounter reinforces the truth that the Holy Spirit shares the knowledge of God with us, revealing the mysteries that only He can know. But for what purpose? Often, He is giving us an opportunity to share God's love, wisdom, and nearness with others in a personal and powerful way.

Spiritual Knowledge Creates Opportunities for Physical Healing

Prophetic messages with knowledge from the Holy Spirit not only create opportunities for faith to rise and the Holy Spirit to bring spiritual healing or encouragement but also create opportunities for physical healing.

I was parked at a Sonic Drive-In picking up dinner for my family when, out of the blue, I thought of a friend I hadn't seen in years. We had been close when we lived near each other, but life, thousands of miles, and a few babies had changed our relationship some. The good news is, she was one of those special friends I could call or text anytime, even if it'd been awhile since we'd been in touch, and we'd pick up right where we left off.

Our relationship has always been low pressure and high value. By that, I mean we never put heavy expectations on each other because life was so busy, but our time together was life-giving.

Everyone deserves a friend like her, and to be honest, I'm blessed enough to have a few.

I opened my text messages as I waited for the carhop to deliver my order and typed a quick note: "Thinking of you today and praying for your health, your heart, and your home (family). Love you."

She replied, "Well, that was very timely. Thank you, friend. Love you." She was far along in pregnancy with her second baby, and as I read her response, I had this picture of her with both arms under her belly, almost like you would cradle a baby. The picture I saw in my head looked like she was in pain. I couldn't ignore it, so I texted, "Are you in pain? I had this picture of you holding the bottom of your belly like a person might cradle a baby. I wondered if maybe you had nerve or back pain?"

She sent back crying emojis and this response: "Yes. I was literally reading this text, holding the bottom of my belly while wearing a belly band because my lower back hurts so much."

Our conversation continued: "Well, I'm agreeing with you right now for the pressure to shift and the pain to go and relief to come now in Jesus' name," I texted. "I can see Him standing at your side facing you with one hand on your belly and one hand on your lower back . . . and at first I thought you were supposed to put a heating pad on your lower back, but I realized there is a healing heat He is releasing right now to relieve the pain."

What I heard next from her was complete joy! She took off the belly band because she had immediate relief. She said it felt as if her belly was lighter, and the pressure she had felt lifted in that instant. She explained that she had just flown back from seeing family, and the flight had really messed with her back. Her husband was sick and highly contagious, so she couldn't go see the chiropractor. She was desperate for relief, and our good and loving God had provided it. We both thanked God for what He had done and gave Jesus the glory for being our Healer.

I believe we often put limits on the supernatural work we believe God can accomplish in and through us. But, my friend, God is so big and so real and so close. As we become awakened to His living presence within us, I can't help but wonder, *What would happen if we believed everything He said was true? What would happen if we really did choose to pause, listen, and look with our spiritual eyes and ears? What would we hear? What would we know? What would God invite us to do together?* It all starts with the decision to take a step of faith.

Taking a Step of Faith

A few years ago I was sitting in a coffee shop, working on writing a previous book, when I noticed a young man I had seen working there in past visits. He wasn't working that afternoon and was sitting rather close by me, having an important phone conversation. I couldn't hear what he was saying, but as he spoke, I saw a picture in my heart.

The Holy Spirit showed me two fields torn apart, and it was like people were trying to restore them with spoons. I could tell the fields had once been one large, fortified formation, but some division had come and split them in two. I then heard the Lord tell me that the people's efforts weren't going to be successful without Him, and only He could reunite the fields back together as one. Then the Lord told me a name: Ryan.

Honestly, the imagery was so powerful and the name I had heard seemed like such a strange afterthought that I believed I had just made up the name in my own head. Confident of the rest of what God had shown me, I decided to turn to the man when he finished his call and share what I had seen.

The man seemed encouraged by what I had shared, but neither of us were quite sure what it meant. I felt a little as though I had missed something and maybe none of what I heard was from God after all. I ended our chat by saying, "I'm sorry. I never introduced myself. I'm Becky Thompson."

"Oh," he answered. "Nice to meet you. I'm Ryan."

I about fell out of my chair. "Ryan?" I shouted, startling everyone in the small space. "Ryan?" I said again, this time a little quieter. "Are you kidding me? God just told me your name was Ryan, and can you imagine how much more personal this would have been if you knew for certain God had meant this message for you? I'm so sorry I didn't ask if your name was Ryan in the beginning."

I learned an important lesson that day. I would always rather say what I believe God told me and be mistaken than hold my tongue and miss an opportunity to prove to someone that God knows their very name.

I remembered this lesson when I was writing this book in a quiet bookstore one afternoon and the Lord prompted me to share something with another woman working nearby. I had a spot in an area that was free from distractions. My home office and coffee shops just weren't working for this book, and I needed to be alone with the Holy Spirit and my thoughts. The chair I enjoyed writing from in the bookstore faced a green space where there was very little activity, and the chairs were spaced far apart because this was during the time of social distancing.

I had been sitting for a while, and I heard the Lord say, "Get up and stretch for a minute." It didn't matter if it was me or Him who had this idea, because honestly, I needed a break. But I did feel as though this prompting was significant and for some specific purpose. As I stood to walk a lap around the room, the Holy Spirit pointed out a woman who was flipping through note cards, studying.

"She's studying for an important test, and she's worried about it. I want you to tell her that I care more about the outcome of that test than she does. She has put off pursuing this education because she was busy taking care of her children, specifically her daughter, but she's not delayed; this is the perfect timing for what will come next."

Then He told me the name: Danielle. It was as if Jesus were walking next to me, telling me something only He knew about His friend. I knew what He wanted me to do, but for some reason, I was nervous to approach her. What if everything I heard was just in my head?

I have found that the Enemy tries to tell me the same lie he told Eve in the garden: "Did God really say?" he questions (Genesis 3:1). To Eve, the Enemy questioned if God really said not to eat the forbidden fruit. To me, he asks, "Did God really say what you think you heard Him say, or are you making it all up?"

Trusting the Spirit and remembering Ryan's story, I decided to approach her. I said, "Hi, I'm sorry. This is pretty awkward, and I promise I'm not asking for anything . . . But I was just having a spiritual moment, and I believe God has something He wants me to tell you. Are you studying for a test?"

"Yes," she answered.

"Do you have a daughter?" She confirmed that she did and looked a little shocked.

"Is it because of your daughter that you haven't pursued what you are pursuing, studying for this test?"

She began to cry.

I told her exactly what God wanted her to know. I told her that God had seen the sacrifices she made for her family and was with her as she studied. He cared so much about what was going to come next for her, whatever it might be, and she didn't have to worry about the outcome of the test. Then I asked, "Is your name Danielle by any chance?"

Her jaw dropped. I just knew that she was going to say yes, but then she answered, "No. It's not, but someone very close to me is named Danielle, and I have been thinking about her so much." I told her that God telling me the name Danielle meant that He was thinking about Danielle too. Their relationship was important to this woman, and God wanted her to know that He hadn't forgotten about Danielle.

She then told me the details of the test she was studying for and how her life came to be the way it was. Everything she shared lined up with what God had shown me. It was less than five minutes of our day, but it reminded us both that there is a very real God who cares very much about us. And it brought us both closer to Him, which is always the purpose of God speaking to us for others.

The truth is, we don't always know why the Holy Spirit asks us to step out in faith and share His love, but every word of knowledge from the Spirit is like a seed from heaven. We simply have to listen to His voice and trust the power of truth to grow into eternal life once seeded into someone else's heart.

> **The truth is, we don't always know why the Holy Spirit asks us to step out in faith and share His love, but every word of knowledge from the Spirit is like a seed from heaven.**

So, I'll ask you: Has God ever spoken to you this way? Did you know this way of knowing Him and His heart was even possible? Let's pray and thank the Holy Spirit for being the God who knows every detail of our lives.

Let's Pray

Father God,

Thank You for all the ways You share Your love with us. We see now that if the Spirit searches all things, even the deep things of Your heart, then we can receive insight that has the potential to transform someone's life. Teach us how to listen for the knowledge You want to reveal. Teach us how to see others as You see them. We understand that this gift isn't for our benefit or for us to boast in. But in all things we acknowledge that we are fully reliant on You to be who You are, and we simply share what You ask us to say.

Right now, we ask You to move in our hearts and give a new measure of understanding to our minds. We want to know all that is possible in a life awakened by Your Spirit. In Jesus' name we pray. Amen.

Let's Reflect

1. Have you ever had a moment when you believed God was telling you something only He could know? What happened?
2. In your own words, how might it encourage a person to realize that God knows the details of her life and has a plan for her?

CHAPTER 13

THE GIFTS OF THE SPIRIT

*Why the Body of Christ
Needs Your Spiritual Gifts*

love a good superhero movie. The idea of some otherworldly power that enables men and women to defeat the forces of darkness? Come on! What's not to love? To be honest, I spend most of my time watching those movies looking for parallels between the screenplay and what I know to be true about the sons and daughters of God who have also been given supernatural authority and power.

A few years ago a series of movies was released by one of the major superhero franchises that changed the game for what fans hoped to see going forward (at least what this fan hoped to see going forward). Whereas most of the previous movies focused on individual heroes, these new movies showed the power of heroes coming together. Separately, they were gifted. Together, they were nearly unstoppable.

Some had superstrength, others had uncommon intelligence. Some were superflexible, and others were superfast. They each had distinguishing powers that, when united, were used for the greater good of their group and those they were called to protect.

As I watched the new teamed-up movies unfold, I thought of Paul's words to the Corinthian church: "Dear brothers and sisters, regarding your question about the special abilities the Spirit gives us. I don't want you to misunderstand this. . . . There are different kinds of spiritual gifts, but the same Spirit is the source of them all. . . . A spiritual gift is given to each of us so we can help each other" (1 Corinthians 12:1, 4, 7 NLT).

I want to be abundantly clear. The group Paul was speaking to wasn't made up of the twelve disciples Jesus taught. This group of Believers had been converted out of paganism and were previously idol worshipers. They had embraced the good news about Jesus and were filled with the Holy Spirit. It was to this group that Paul gave instructions on how to use their new supernatural gifts. Look carefully again at those words Paul said to them at the end of that last statement: "A spiritual gift is given to each of us so we can help each other."

Paul's emphasis in this passage wasn't an attempt to convince the church that they were in possession of the gifts; they already knew the spiritual gifts existed. His aim was to encourage them to honor the Spirit who gives the gifts and to use the gifts for their intended purpose—building up the body of Christ.

He then listed a collection of supernatural giftings:

To one person the Spirit gives the ability to give wise advice; to another the same Spirit gives a message of special knowledge. The same Spirit gives great faith to another, and to someone else the one Spirit gives the gift of healing. He gives one person the power to perform miracles, and another the ability to prophesy. He gives someone else the ability to discern whether a message is from the Spirit of God or from another spirit. Still another person is given the ability to speak in unknown languages, while another is given the ability to interpret what is being said. It is the one and only Spirit who distributes all these gifts. He alone decides which gift each person should have. (vv. 8–11 NLT)

Paul went on to explain that the spiritual gifts are like parts of a body—needed for the whole to function properly. He questioned,

> If the whole body were an eye, how would you hear? Or if your whole body were an ear, how would you smell anything?
>
> But our bodies have many parts, and God has put each part just where he wants it. How strange a body would be if it had only one part! Yes, there are many parts, but only one body. The eye can never say to the hand, "I don't need you." The head can't say to the feet, "I don't need you." . . .
>
> All of you together are Christ's body, and each of you is a part of it. (vv. 17–21, 27 NLT)

What Paul told the Corinthians is true for us today. The spiritual gifts are given to all Believers just as the Spirit is given to all Believers; the giftings are His work moving through us. The Holy Spirit hasn't changed, so the gifts haven't changed. Our spiritual gifts don't come when we become aware of them. Our gifts come when the Holy Spirit fills us. Do you see what that means, friend? You have spiritual gifts that the Holy Spirit wants to teach you more about! And it's okay to still be learning about them.

Paul sent letters to multiple churches about the gifts of the Spirit and how to use them. They had received spiritual gifts, but they still needed instruction about them. This teaches us that God wants us to use our spiritual gifts properly in the body of Christ today.

The problem is, not all Believers know they are in possession of these gifts from the Spirit. They don't know they've been given the ability to prophesy or teach. They don't know the Holy Spirit has given them supernatural knowledge or faith. And what good are our Holy Spirit superpowers to the body of Christ, the Church, if we don't even know we have them? Let's learn more about what we are in possession of and how to wield these tools.

Supernatural Gifts in the Old Testament

Throughout Scripture the Holy Spirit gave special abilities and giftings to men and women to accomplish God's purposes. We see these moments in the New Testament, but the Holy Spirit was present and moving among God's people long before Jesus was born. In the Old Testament, the Holy Spirit had not yet been poured out on all flesh, but He did fill select men and women with His power, wisdom, knowledge, and special abilities for specific purposes and for temporary periods of time. Each instance when the Spirit gave these giftings, He did so to use regular men and women like you and me to carry out God's perfect plan.

Bezalel—Filled with the Spirit's Wisdom

Do you remember how we discussed the cloud of God's presence, which descended on the tabernacle, the moveable structure the Israelites followed as the cloud moved wherever He led them? There's a story about a man named Bezalel, a skilled craftsman, to whom the Holy Spirit gifted wisdom to know how to build this house for God's presence. A blueprint given by heavenly insight would definitely require supernatural wisdom to build, don't you suppose?

Exodus 31:1–5 tells us, "The LORD said to Moses, 'See, I have chosen Bezalel son of Uri, the son of Hur, of the tribe of Judah, and I have filled him with the Spirit of God, with wisdom, with understanding, with knowledge and with all kinds of skills—to make artistic designs for work in gold, silver and bronze, to cut and set stones, to work in wood, and to engage in all kinds of crafts.'"

Do you know what I love about this? The Lord told Moses that Bezalel had received supernatural wisdom. Bezalel wasn't just a guy who knew what to do because he had years of practice or earthly academics. He had been chosen by God and given supernatural ability that came through the power of the Holy Spirit. Moses didn't have to wonder who to put in charge of this important task, or question whether Bezalel was making the right choices or carrying out this work in the right way. God appointed Bezalel and affirmed His appointment.

Essentially, God told Moses, "Bezalel is doing My work as if I were doing it Myself." In this instance, God gave supernatural insight (which a human mind wouldn't previously have) and His divine creativity (which God Himself displayed when He made the earth) to Bezalel so he could make the very specific details of the tabernacle. What a gift to the group! But also, what a gift for Bezalel to know the Spirit of God in such a personal and powerful way!

Gideon—Clothed with the Spirit

There is another story in Scripture about a man named Gideon who had the gift of wisdom from the Spirit. Many years after Bezalel crafted the tabernacle, the Israelites turned away from worshiping God, and, as a result, their enemies had overcome them. But God had a plan. To defeat the invading armies and turn the hearts of His people back toward Him, God gave a man named Gideon a divine strategy.

He told Gideon what to do, and at the right moment, "The Spirit of the LORD *came upon* Gideon; then he blew the trumpet, and the Abiezrites gathered behind him" (Judges 6:34 NKJV). What's so special about that? The Hebrew word translated "came upon" here means "put on, wear, clothe, be clothed."[1] It was as if the Holy Spirit *wore* Gideon and moved through him. Talk about God So Close!

> **If God is going to use ordinary people to accomplish His extraordinary work, then it will require His supernatural presence and participation.**

The truth is, if God is going to use ordinary people to accomplish His extraordinary work, then it will require His supernatural presence and participation. *We can do nothing for God apart from God* (John 15:5). This has always been true. (Now, I'm just saying . . . I'd go back and underline that.)

Spiritual Gifts Today

So what, if anything, has changed about the Spirit's supernatural giftings since these events in Scripture took place? The Spirit Himself hasn't changed, but the human relationship with Him has become even closer through the sacrifice of Jesus.

We've talked about it again and again in this book. You and I know that Jesus made it possible for the Spirit to fill *all* Believers rather than a select few. As the prophet Joel foretold, God said someday He would give His Spirit to *all* people. Look at the people He listed: "I will pour out my Spirit upon all people. Your sons and daughters will prophesy. Your old men will dream dreams, and your young men will see visions. In those days I will pour out my Spirit even on servants—men and women alike" (Joel 2:28–29 NLT).

The focus of that passage of Scripture is *all*. When the day of Pentecost came and all those gathered in the upper room were filled with the Holy Spirit, Peter declared, "What you see was predicted long ago by the prophet Joel: 'In the last days,' God says, 'I will pour out my Spirit upon *all* people'" (Acts 2:16–17 NLT). This outpouring remains available for all who accept Jesus.

If Peter said the time had come for all Believers to have the Spirit and that the Spirit gives supernatural abilities, then we must remember we're in possession of what only a select few people experienced in ancient times. We have the Spirit who gives us gifts. What are these gifts, and how do we use them exactly? Let's see what else Paul taught.

The Proper Use of Spiritual Gifts

Paul didn't speak only to the Corinthian church about the gifts of the Spirit. He also sent word to those in the Roman church. I think it's significant to note that Paul spoke to the Roman church about the spiritual gifts even though he had yet to visit this congregation of Believers. This shows us that he had either received word that they had experienced the gifts of the Spirit, or more likely, he presupposed they had. If he assumed they had experienced these spiritual gifts, then that tells us what Paul believed was the standard. If you profess to follow Christ, then you have received His Spirit. And if you have received His Spirit, then you know He moves in spiritual giftings.

This is what Paul said to the Roman church about spiritual gifts:

> As we have many members in one body, but all the members do not have the same function, so we, being many, are one body in Christ, and individually members of one another. Having then gifts differing according to the grace that is given to us, let us use them: if prophecy, let us prophesy in proportion to our faith; or ministry, let us use it in our ministering; he who teaches, in teaching; he who exhorts, in exhortation; he who gives, with liberality; he who leads, with diligence; he who shows mercy, with cheerfulness. (Romans 12:4–8 NKJV)

Notice that Paul's focus on spiritual gifts here is the same as in his letter to the Corinthian believers. It is to teach their proper use of the spiritual gifts in the body of Christ, the Church. The truth is, spiritual gifts are given to us, but they aren't just for us. They are given so that we can impact others. They are given for the health of the whole group.

Spiritual Gifts Are Tools, Not Toys

There's a story written by renowned author C. S. Lewis that paints a beautiful allegory of what happens when sons and daughters of God use what He has given them for the glory of their King.

In Lewis's classic novel *The Lion, the Witch and the Wardrobe,* young Lucy Pevensie discovers a portal to a magical kingdom called Narnia, and learns that she and her three siblings are the foretold kings and queens of that realm. When Lucy and her siblings arrive in Narnia, they encounter an evil queen who has placed Narnia under her power. But alongside the great king Aslan, Lucy and her siblings defeat the witch and restore peace to the kingdom.

A great theologian, author, and professor, C. S. Lewis created this story to help young readers understand how the Great King (Jesus) has defeated the evil ruler (Satan), and we as God's appointed coheirs with Jesus (the children) have authority in the world that He made and purchased back with the sacrifice of His own life.

I highly recommend reading this book. It is full of underlinable quotes, which you know I love. But there is one part of this story I especially love, and I thought of it again and again as I prepared to write this chapter.

The story goes that as three of the children travel through the woods to meet with Aslan, they encounter Father Christmas, who bears gifts for all. The gifts presented to each child, one by one, isn't meant only for that child. The siblings will use their gifts together to defeat their enemy, help the inhabitants of Narnia, and complete the task given to them by Aslan, their king.

To Lucy's oldest brother, Peter, Father Christmas gives a sword and a shield. To her older sister, Susan, Father Christmas gives a bow and arrow and a horn to blow with the understanding that when she calls, help will come. To Lucy, Father Christmas gives a small dagger and a diamond bottle containing a cordial useful for healing.

All these gifts are given by Father Christmas with instructions on how and when to use them. To Peter, he says, "These are your presents, and they are tools, not toys. The time to use them is perhaps near at hand. Bear them well."[2]

Tools, not toys. I get shivers when I read that because I believe I know what Lewis was attempting to illustrate with this portion of the story. Father Christmas represents the Holy Spirit, who also gives gifts that are tools, not toys, meant for the good of all. While we might enjoy the gifts we've been given, and while it might seem fun to prophesy or share a word of knowledge or perhaps serve joyfully, we also must learn to bear these tools well and use them to care for the kingdom.

Practical Applications of Spiritual Gifts

Let's think about this for just a moment and translate these spiritual ideas into practical ones.

Last year, after my grandfather passed away, my parents became the caretakers of my grandmother and her estate. She wanted to live in an assisted living community that she and my grandfather had toured before his death. When moving to this new home, my grandmother chose to start over and leave many of her things behind. I admire her outlook and determination to move forward even without her beloved husband.

Back at her house, however, my parents were left with the tasks of sorting through a lifetime's worth of belongings and preparing the house to be sold. There was much to be done, and my mom did what she does best. With her own spiritual gift of administration, she was able to organize the flow of contractors, painters, appraisers, real estate agents, foundation repairmen, movers, and professional cleaners. Each one brought their own skill set to the project and were able to make the overwhelming tasks of sorting through all that was left behind and selling the house achievable.

My parents didn't need painters who tried to repair the foundation. They didn't need real estate agents who tried to paint the house. They didn't need cleaners who attempted to fix the drywall. My parents needed each group of helpers to show up and do what they do best so the entire project could be completed.

This is how it should be among Believers of Jesus. In the previous chapters, I've told you some of my stories about instances when God asked me to prophesy or share knowledge from God's heart or have faith for a friend to be healed. I shared about how these moments impacted my life, but in these stories it's clear that God touched those on the other side of these encounters. We must remember our giftings are for us so they can be used through us.

The spiritual gifts are not just for our own enjoyment. They aren't presents for us to boast in. They are meant to impact the people Jesus wants to touch and speak to; He simply invites our hands, hearts, minds, and voices to be part of His process. As a result, those on the other side of our obedience are touched by the Holy Spirit. The blessing we receive from using these gifts is the relationship we have with the Holy Spirit as we allow Him to move through us.

> We must remember our giftings are for us so they can be used through us.

To date, this book is my eighth published work. Some of the most encouraging feedback I have received over the years from those who've read my previous books is this: "I feel like this was written just for me! How did you know I needed to hear that? It was like I was reading my own thoughts."

I'm going to tell you something embarrassing. When I first received those messages, I truly believed that I must be a gifted storyteller, and writing books was something I was meant to do. Some people are good doctors and others are good lawyers, and I thought I was just someone who understands how some women think, and I write about it. It wasn't until one afternoon as I was thinking about how I had been asked, "How did you know that I needed to hear that?" that the Holy Spirit answered, *You didn't until I showed you.*

It had always been Him. Yes, I listened well. I shared well. But it was the hope of Jesus, His insight, and His knowledge of what was needed just when it was needed that did the healing heart work. This is how these spiritual gifts flow through us and not just to us. We are fountains, not pools, and the source of what we offer is the "living water" Jesus spoke of in His conversation with the Samaritan woman at the well (John 4:10).

The Body of Christ Is Counting on You!

Believe me when I tell you the world needs your spiritual gifts. People in your life need you to show up carrying the power of the Holy Spirit, who is inside of you, and to allow Him to work through you in supernatural ways. This is how Jesus is made real to others as the Holy Spirit moves through you. This is what distinguishes you as a Believer from all those in the world who are still lost and looking.

My friend, the team is counting on you. The body of Christ

needs your feet, your hands, your mouth, and your heart. We are incomplete without you! Can someone else do what you can do? Yes, God will accomplish His purposes no matter what. But don't miss this: You have an invitation not simply to watch others experience the power of the Holy Spirit but to be one who says, "Here I am, Lord, send me, use me, flow through me!"

Just as being filled with the Holy Spirit isn't something we work for, His giftings aren't something we achieve. But they do require Spirit-led participation on our end. We must know we have them. We must decide that we want to use them. And then we must boldly yield to the Spirit who wants to flow through us.

Jesus wants to touch the world, and He's asking for your hands to do it.

Let's Pray

Father God,

Thank You for the spiritual gifts You've given us. We recognize that they aren't toys, but tools. They give us the opportunity to love others and know You in a more intimate way.

We pause to look back at our lives, and we ask, "Were there moments when You 'wore' us as You wore Gideon, or filled us with wisdom as You filled Bezalel?" Surely Your Spirit has been at work in our lives even before we knew it was Him.

Now we ask, "What can we do together? What giftings have You given us so that the world may experience the relationship with Jesus we have experienced?" We want to be a part of what You are doing, Lord. Teach us how to carry Your power with grace. In Jesus' name we pray. Amen.

Let's Reflect

1. Open your Bible to Romans 12:6–8 and 1 Corinthians 12:8–10, 28–30 and look at the gifts Paul mentioned. Which ones do you see evident in your own life?

2. In your own words, why does the body of Christ need you to remember you are a Spirit-filled Believer?

CHAPTER 14

THE PURSUIT OF GOD

What Do You Seek?

W hat do you seek?"

This is the first question that Jesus asked His first disciples (John 1:38 NKJV), and though it's a simple one, it held more meaning than you might expect.

A man named John, Jesus' cousin, had been announcing to all those who would listen that the promised Messiah was coming. John was wild—I mean, he was "eating locusts and honey and dressed in furs" kind of wild. Weird. I can only imagine what people thought of John. In his unwavering determination to tell of the coming Christ, John had gathered a crowd.

Jewish men, who knew from prophecies that one day a Savior would be born and rescue their people from persecution, came to listen to John. For centuries, this coming King had been foretold. However, no one expected the Savior to come from a small town like Nazareth, and they certainly didn't expect Him to look or sound or act like Jesus did. Yet John knew that his cousin was the promised Christ.

One day while John was teaching, Jesus walked toward him and John declared, "Behold! The Lamb of God who takes away the sin of the world!" (John 1:29 NKJV). Two men who heard John say this followed Jesus as He began to walk past.

I like to wonder what else was going on at this moment. What did these two men say to each other as they walked behind Him? Did one whisper to the other, "What if John is right, and this man really is our Messiah?" Scripture says the two of them "followed Jesus" (v. 37), but were they following with a big crowd or sneaking along behind Jesus, wondering if He'd notice?

There are many details not included in Scripture's account of this story, but I personally believe that as these two men walked behind Jesus, there was likely more than curiosity stirring. After all, Jesus said, "No one can come to me unless the Father who sent me draws them" (John 6:44). It was the Father who'd pulled at their hearts and caused them to pursue Jesus that day, even if they weren't aware of it. Maybe they just thought they were going to see if there was any truth to John's words.

When Jesus saw them following Him, He turned and asked, "What do you seek?" (John 1:38 NKJV). Notice what He didn't say? There was no, "Hello, fellas. Nice day. Beautiful weather. I'm Jesus. It's nice to meet you." He spoke immediately to the point and to their hearts: "What do you seek?"

Can we acknowledge for just a second that Jesus already knew the answer to this question? As God, Jesus knew their intentions. He also knew that one of these men, Andrew, would be the very first person chosen to aid in the completion of His perfect rescue plan (even though in this moment Andrew had no idea). Yet Jesus still greeted them with this profound question: "What do you seek?"

He gave both men a chance to define exactly what they were hoping to find. Scripture records that they replied, "Rabbi . . . , where are You staying?" (v. 38 NKJV). And Jesus answered, "Come and see" (v. 39 NKJV).

You know, I believe these men sought what our hearts desire as well. Yes, we are curious if God really is who He says He is, and we want it to be true. But ultimately we want to know God for ourselves and to be the friends invited to follow Him. We seek more than information; we want relationship.

Why Do You Follow Jesus?

I wonder, if Jesus were to turn and ask us the same question He asked those two followers, what would we say? Why *do* you follow Him? Do you just want to know more about the life He offers you or what the Holy Spirit makes available to you? Or do you purely want to be with Him because you want to know Him as fully as you can? I promise they are two entirely different pursuits, but only one will satisfy what our hearts crave.

I deeply believe we all long to have what was once available in the garden of Eden. We want an unhindered relationship with God. We want to talk with Him as a friend and be free from the things that would try to separate us. We want to know God in His fullness. But we attempt to satisfy our search for intimacy with a search for information. My friend, only one of those two things converts into heart food. Many of us are starving spiritually, but we don't realize it because we know Jesus and His Word, and we are doing everything we think we are supposed to do as Christians.

We feel stressed, overwhelmed, anxious (hello, raising my hand!), short-tempered, confused, depressed, or hopeless. So we attempt to relax, unwind, create peace, reduce stress, seek direction, find joy, or create moments to look forward to and stir hope. But deep down we are hungry for God's presence. We are hungry for what only He can provide. We are hungry for the change that can happen in us only when He comes close. But I'm afraid we don't even recognize our pains as hunger anymore.

When my kids were little, they'd get super cranky when they were hungry. They came by it honestly; I get cranky when I'm hungry too. You could tell when it was almost lunch or dinnertime because they seemed more emotional. If a toy didn't work correctly, they'd cry. If one of them didn't share with the other, they'd cry. If they were given a blue cup instead of a green one, they'd cry.

They couldn't necessarily communicate, "You know, I think I'd feel better if I had a meal. I think I need a piece of fruit or some protein to sort out what's really bothering me." So they'd just feel frustrated or upset or as if everything wasn't quite going their way until we got to the root of the problem. They might be crying for what they thought was one reason, but the cause was something entirely different. They just needed to be fed.

Come to Jesus

There is an event recorded in John's gospel where Jesus was talking with a crowd who was also hungry. He had just fed them miraculously. Thousands had come to listen to Him teach, and He didn't want to send them away to eat. So He had taken a small offering of bread and fish and supernaturally multiplied it. When people began talking about this miraculous event, He said,

> "It is my Father who gives you the true bread from heaven. For the bread of God is the bread that comes down from heaven and gives life to the world."

"Sir," they said, "always give us this bread."

Then Jesus declared, "I am the bread of life. Whoever comes to me will never go hungry, and whoever believes in me will never be thirsty." (John 6:32–35)

What I love about this story is that Jesus didn't send these people away to have their practical needs met after He'd been meeting their spiritual needs. The people came to Him for their hearts, and they left with full hearts and full bellies because Jesus knew the two were connected.

When we come to Jesus, we find not just what our spirits need but also provision for every area of and situation in our lives.

Your child is sick? *Come to Jesus.*

Your bills need paying? *Come to Jesus.*

Your marriage is in shambles? *Come to Jesus.*

Your employer isn't honoring your work? *Come to Jesus.*

You need strength? Hope? Wisdom? Power? Encouragement? Joy? Peace? Patience? Kindness? Goodness? Faithfulness? Gentleness? Self-control? *Come to Jesus.*

Jesus is continually inviting us, "Come. Take and eat. Come to Me, and you'll never go hungry." And we answer, "Of course! We'd love to!" But do we? Do we understand what it looks like to find nourishment for our hearts in the presence of God? Because information about Jesus doesn't fuel us; *He* does. Knowledge isn't the gift. *His Spirit within us* who gives us knowledge is the gift.

Notice that Jesus didn't say, "Whoever talks about Me" or "Whoever hears about Me" will never go hungry. He didn't say, "Whoever attends church regularly," or "Whoever reads books about Me," or "Whoever listens to podcasts about Me," or "Whoever follows faith-focused Instagrammers" will never go hungry. He didn't even say, "Whoever knows the most about Me will never go hungry." No. He said, "I am the bread of life. Whoever *comes to me* will never go hungry."

The Pursuit of God versus the Pursuit of Knowledge

A question I have asked myself frequently during the last decade of writing and leading women is this: Have we stopped chasing after God Himself and replaced our pursuit of Him with the pursuit of information about Him?

Take just a second and read that again: *Have we stopped chasing after God Himself and replaced our pursuit of Him with the pursuit of information about Him?*

For so many, I believe the answer is yes. Not intentionally, of course! Perhaps we simply didn't know just what kind of intimacy with God was available to us. The truth is, information about God is good, but it doesn't satisfy the longing that only His presence can. Don't get me wrong: It's important to read the Word so we know God's voice and commands. It's important to meditate on what He has said and then actually do it. The Word of God is daily bread, but it doesn't come alive in our minds. It comes alive in our spirits, so it requires the presence of the Holy Spirit to help us consume it and nourish our hearts with it.

Either the Holy Spirit reveals Jesus to us, or we just know *about* Him. We can know Him only as He is revealed by the Spirit. Anyone can read the Bible as a letter written by a faraway

God and never have an encounter with Him, a moment when He becomes more than facts—He becomes a Father.

Am I questioning your salvation? No! I am saying that our intellect is not what must be changed for us to be born again. Minds can be changed and changed again. Our spirits must be transformed by His Spirit for us to be born again. God does not intend to convince you He is real. He intends to *show* you He is.

This is why it is so important that we remember that "the person without the Spirit does not accept the things that come from the Spirit of God but considers them foolishness, and cannot understand them because they are discerned only through the Spirit" (1 Corinthians 2:14). We need the Spirit of God within us in order to understand anything about God for ourselves.

We need the Spirit of God within us in order to understand anything about God for ourselves.

Spending time learning is valuable, but we cannot forget that the Father gave us His Word, His Son, and His Spirit so that we could find our way back to Him. I'll say it again: *God is the prize of all that we seek.* From the beginning of time, however, the Enemy has attempted to keep us from encountering God by replacing our pursuit of Him with the pursuit of knowledge. Here's what I mean.

When God made Adam and Eve and placed them in the garden of Eden at the beginning of creation, they had perfect access to God. They walked with Him and spoke with Him. There was nothing that hindered their relationship with Him in the garden, and this is how He intended it to be for all eternity.

But you might remember that in the garden there were two specific trees: the Tree of Life and the Tree of Knowledge of

Good and Evil. Now, these were more than metaphorical trees. These were actual trees with actual fruit. Eating the fruit from one tree offered eternal life. Eating the fruit from the other tree brought the knowledge of good and evil. God commanded Adam and Eve, "You are free to eat from any tree in the garden; but you must not eat from the tree of the knowledge of good and evil, for when you eat from it you will certainly die" (Genesis 2:16–17).

I need to point something out here. Adam and Eve had never experienced death or deceit. Evil was completely foreign to them. They didn't even know that someone could deceive them because they only knew goodness. They only knew the perfection into which God had placed them. They only knew how to trust. And it was because Eve only knew how to trust that, when the serpent spoke to her as she walked close to the forbidden tree one day, she trusted him when he said that the fruit was good.

Do you remember the details of this story? The Enemy of our hearts, in the form of a serpent, told Eve, "You will not certainly die [if you eat the fruit from this tree]. . . . For God knows that when you eat from it your eyes will be opened, and you will be like God, knowing good and evil" (3:4–5). And do you know what she did? Eve trusted the serpent when he told her that eating from the Tree of Knowledge of Good and Evil would make her like God.

Eve elevated the serpent's voice over God's in her heart, and all her descendants suffered the consequences of her decision. But I want to pause for a second because there's a point here I'm trying to help us to see. What was the name of the tree that the Enemy used to lure Eve away?

It was the Tree of *Knowledge* of Good and Evil. Genesis records that when Eve saw that the tree was "desirable for gaining wisdom" (v. 6), she chose to eat. Look here, friend. The Enemy told Eve that she would be like God if she ate from the Tree of Knowledge of Good and Evil, but this was deceitful because she was already like God.

Genesis 1:26 says that Eve was made in God's image, in His likeness. From her formation, she was already like her Creator. All she needed to do to remain like Him was to stay in His presence by following His command. But by taking Satan's bait, Eve made an exchange. And do you see what she chose? Eve chose the pursuit of wisdom and knowledge rather than choosing to continue to pursue the presence of her Father.

Today, I'm afraid that many of us still exchange intimacy for knowledge. We eat from the tree of knowledge and information rather than from the Tree of Life. We seek to become like God by learning more about Him rather than believing He wants to come close to us and transform us into His likeness by the power of His presence.

We can no more make ourselves like God by reading about Him than we can make ourselves like a bird by reading about birds. A miraculous transformation in us will happen only when the Spirit of Jesus comes and abides in us, giving us the mind of Christ (1 Corinthians 2:16) and filling us "with all joy and peace in believing" (Romans 15:13 NKJV). Then, by the power of the Holy Spirit, we will be raised to new life and cry out to God our Father as His daughters.

> We can no more make ourselves like God by reading about Him than we can make ourselves like a bird by reading about birds.

An Invitation to Carry His Power and Love

My friend, my prayer for you from the beginning of this book has been that reading these words would not merely be informative but would stir in you a desire for your own encounters with His Holy Spirit. I prayed that it would offer invitations for your heart to become awakened by Him.

In these chapters, you've learned who the Holy Spirit is in Scripture. You've learned about His holiness and perfection and how He manifests His presence. You've been awakened to His voice, His power, His gifts, and His leading. There is a supernatural life available for you. But no amount of information, no matter how Spirit-filled, is going to satisfy what only His living presence can.

The Holy Spirit reveals Jesus, who is the Bread of Life, the Living Water, the First and the Last, the King of kings, and the one and only Son of God . . . and we must decide why we pursue Him daily.

So listen closely, listen with your heart, as the same Spirit who raised Jesus from the dead and who now lives in you asks, "What do you seek? Why do you follow Me? What are you hoping to discover?" And know that He invites you to be not only a follower but also a carrier of His power and love.

My friend, there are people waiting for you to manifest the Holy Spirit in your relationships, communities, churches, schools, and businesses. There are people who will encounter Jesus for the first time as His Spirit works through you. I pray for you as Paul prayed for Timothy. I pray that God would help you "fan into flame the gift of God. . . . For the Spirit God gave us does not make us timid, but gives us power, love and self-discipline. . . . He has saved us and called us to a holy life—not because of anything we have done but because of his own purpose and grace" (2 Timothy 1:6–7, 9).

There's More for You!

Before you go, I'll remind you of what I said at the beginning of our time together, since our mission doesn't end here but continues on. Let's ask the Holy Spirit to meet with us and explain to us spiritual things that foolish people cannot understand. Let's break free from believing the Enemy's lies about what God can't do. And let's go to His Word, looking at who the Holy Spirit reveals Himself to be and what our response to Him should look like. Let's bravely consider the power of a life awakened by His Spirit.

I believe that no matter how close God has been to you in the past, there's a deeper, closer, and even more familiar experience available to you. No matter how much you know about Him, there's more to discover because He is infinite. There are no borders of the great expanse of God's being. And day by day, moment by moment, He is inviting you deeper into His heart.

Day by day, He remains God So Close.

Let's Pray

Father God,

We know that You have been the one leading our hearts toward Yours. We see now that it has always been Your

Spirit—the Spirit who filled Your Son, the Spirit of truth— who has been calling us into a relationship with You.

We mark this moment as the one where we said we don't just want to have information about You. We want to encounter Your Spirit in whatever way You make available to us.

Daily ask us, "What do you seek?" so we can reaffirm the purpose of why we follow You. Continually fill us with Your Holy Spirit. Open our spiritual eyes and ears to the world around us so we can share the love of Christ. Tune our hearts to Yours. We don't want to go anywhere unless You go with us. Help us desire Your spiritual giftings so we can show the world Your love.

Thank You for meeting us here, God. Thank You for awakening our hearts to Your Spirit. Thank You for being God So Close. In Jesus' name we pray. Amen.

Let's Reflect

Just as we began our journey, let's revisit the same questions we pondered at the beginning, writing down who we know the Holy Spirit to be today.

1. Today, when I think of the Holy Spirit, I think of Him as . . .
2. When I think of the power God has given me, the first thing that comes to mind is . . .

Circle these True/False statements with your understanding today:

True or False   The Holy Spirit is a person.

True or False   The Holy Spirit speaks directly to Believers in Jesus today.

True or False   The Holy Spirit fills Believers in Jesus today, supplying supernatural power and wisdom.

True or False   The Holy Spirit gives spiritual gifts to Believers in Jesus today.

ACKNOWLEDGMENTS

To my husband, Jared: I continue to be so grateful for your love and your support of all of my work. You've always done your best to help create room in our busy lives and schedules for me to write. The lives will be impacted by this book because you helped make it possible. I am thankful and I love you!

To my kids, Kolton, Kadence, and Jaxton: Momma loves you! (That's the first thing I want you to read when you flip to the back of this book someday.) You are so loved. My prayer for each of you since before you were even born was that you would meet Jesus at a young age and follow Him all the days of your life. I prayed that you would be filled with the Holy Spirit and know God personally. I'm so thankful that God has answered my prayers. I'm so blessed to be your momma.

To my parents, Mark and Susan Pitts: Thank you for introducing me to the Holy Spirit and welcoming Him into our home. I am so grateful that you raised me to know and love the Lord. I can share truth in this book because I know it for myself. I'm blessed to be your daughter. I honor who you are as parents and as pastors.

To my friend, Natasha Clark: I'm so grateful that the Lord

sent you to be a friend and encourager in both my life and ministry! I acknowledge the time, effort, and prayer you've given to support me and the women the Lord has brought for me to lead. You are such a joy and truly a gift to know.

To all those who pioneered before me: I want to acknowledge that there have been many who have gone before me, ministering, speaking, and writing books about the Holy Spirit. Their work changed my life, and it is because of their faithfulness that I can continue in the work they began.

To all those who walk alongside me in ministry (there are too many to name, but you know who you are): I'm so grateful that the Lord has called us to follow Him and lead others into deeper Truth. Because of your friendship, your prayer, your encouragement, and your faithfulness to what He has given you to do, this road isn't lonely. The fields are full of my friends who recognize the harvest and set out to bring it in. I love pioneering with you.

To my W Publishing team: Thank you for the space and permission to write exactly what God has placed on my heart. There is no greater gift for a creative than for someone to say, "I trust you and your abilities." You've given support, grace, and the constant reminder that what is said here matters. Thank you for seeing value in what the Lord has given me to say.

And to my agent, Lisa Jackson: Thank you for always being in my corner. I'm grateful to be a part of the Alive family, and I know that the Lord placed me here. We've touched many lives together, following the Lord on this journey. Thank you for your constant support.

NOTES

Chapter 2: The Promise of the Father

1. James Strong, *The New Strong's Expanded Exhaustive Concordance of the Bible* (Nashville, TN: Thomas Nelson, 2010), 205.
2. *Strong's Concordance*, s.v. "243. allos," Bible Hub, accessed September 27, 2021, https://biblehub.com/greek/243.htm.
3. James Strong, "Greek Dictionary of the New Testament," *New Strong's Expanded Exhaustive Concordance of the Bible: Red Letter Edition* (Nashville, TN: Thomas Nelson, 2010), 15.

Chapter 3: The Breath of God

1. *Strong's Concordance*, s.v. "7307. ruach," Bible Hub, accessed September 27, 2021, https://biblehub.com/hebrew/7307.htm.

Chapter 4: The Holiness of God

1. *Strong's Concordance*, s.v. "6942. qadash," Bible Hub, accessed September 27, 2021, https://biblehub.com/hebrew/6942.htm.
2. *Strong's Concordance*, s.v. "6918. qadosh," Bible Hub, accessed September 27, 2021, https://biblehub.com/hebrew/6918.htm.

Chapter 5: The Holy Fire of God

1. *Merriam-Webster*, s.v. "manifest," accessed August 30, 2021, https://www.merriam-webster.com/dictionary/manifest.
2. Exact source unidentified, but Michael Brown has agreed this is

something he has said and has given permission to attribute this quote to him.

Chapter 6: The Outpouring of the Holy Spirit

1. A. W. Tozer, *Life in the Spirit* (Peabody, MA: Hendrickson, 2009), 94.
2. "Ephesians 5:18-19 Commentary," Precept Austin, last updated April 10, 2021, https://www.preceptaustin.org/ephesians _517-18#5:18.

Chapter 13: The Gifts of the Spirit

1. *Strong's Concordance*, s.v. "3847. labash or labesh," Bible Hub, accessed September 27, 2021, https://biblehub.com/hebrew /3847.htm.
2. C. S. Lewis, *The Lion, the Witch and the Wardrobe* (1950; repr., New York: HarperCollins, 2004), 159.

ABOUT THE AUTHOR

Becky Thompson is a bestselling author and the creator of the Midnight Mom Devotional community, where over one million moms gather online in nightly prayer. She and her husband, Jared, live in Northwest Oklahoma with their three children.

GOD LOVES YOU SO MUCH THAT HE MADE A WAY FOR YOU TO BE TOGETHER WITH HIM ALWAYS.

Now He invites you to a deeper and closer relationship with Him.

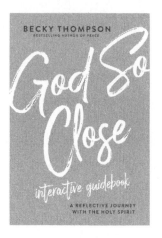

Take a more personal journey through **God So Close** using the **God So Close Interactive Guidebook**, which includes:

- fourteen sessions that cover the entire *God So Close* book
- additional Scripture lessons and new stories
- specific questions to help you reflect on who the Holy Spirit is to you

Will you come discover a life awakened to Him?
Will you get to know God so close?